CIVILIZATION IS NOT YET CIVILIZED

To Kay
A Long time Friend
and fellow Traveler
on this Spiritual path
David Cook

David Cook

ISBN: 1978043554
ISBN 13: 9781978043558
Library of Congress Control Number: 2017916410
CreateSpace Independent Publishing Platform
North Charleston, South Carolina

Since before time and space were,
The Tao is. It is beyond "is" and "is not."
How do I know this is true?
I look inside myself and see.

—Lao Tzu, 500 BC

Do you know human affairs so well
That you are ready to meddle with
those of Heaven?

—Socrates, 400 BC

Man's experience is an optical delusion
of his consciousness.

—Albert Einstein

What we call real time is just a figment of
Our imaginations; it exists only in our minds.

—Stephen Hawking

THE AUTHOR'S NOTE

Giving a physical object to someone means I have to lose in order for that person to gain.

In contrast, if I share a meaningful thought with someone, the person gains the thought while I simultaneously retain the thought. There is no loss; everyone gains, and the thought grows.

There is little of my own wisdom in this book. My thoughts have been shaped by hundreds of authors, teachers, and friends. To name them all is impossible; to name a select few would be an injustice.

A healing message has been passed from century to century by teachable students. I am merely a link in that chain of teachables, and I am grateful for every one of them.

I am not a skillful writer, but I am a reliable messenger because of their sharing.

THE AUTHOR'S HISTORY

I was born in 1940. My early years were challenging. Life in subsidized housing ended at age ten when my father, a veteran of the Second World War, worked six days a week in order to move our family into a modest tract home in a working-class neighborhood. Adjusting to this normal, safe environment took time. From age seventeen to fifty, my employment was blue collar. My extended education began at age fifty when I attended Capital University where I completed a bachelor's degree in social work and went on to receive a master's degree in clinical social work from Ohio State University.

I was employed at a County Mental Health Agency, where I specialized in drug and alcohol treatment. Other areas of practice included anger management training for court-ordered domestic violence clients. My primary method of therapy was solution focused and included relational issues, interpersonal communication, and the additional areas of psychiatric diagnosis. I retired at age sixty-five and continued working for three years at the same agency as a part-time contract therapist.

I live in a small cottage that I built in the middle of six acres of wooded serenity where I read and write. I am active in the Native American community. My Inipi songs are in Lakota, although my ancestors were from other nations. Socializing with and encouraging my friends in the twelve-step community is a special enjoyment.

INTRODUCTION

Everything begins with a thought; the sequence is logical. Thinking leads to behavior, and behavior leads to outcome. We begin with a thought in our mind that manifests as a tangible, material outcome. The Eifel Tower began as a thought before it became a physical structure.

This book is my attempt to explore the thoughts that manifest as tangible, human conflict. I believe that it is a serious misdiagnosis to suggest that war begins with belligerent behavior. Confrontation and war begin with conflicting thoughts. And until we examine the cause or source of those thoughts, there will be no logical solution for curtailing conflict and war. This is also the core reason why civilization is not yet civilized.

When a famous Teacher said, "There will be wars and rumors of wars," he was making a logical observation of human thinking; the erroneous belief that judgment and attack can result in peace. This conclusion was based on his observation of misdirected thinking.

When occasional Peace Teachers appear at select times in history, their message is not greeted with appreciation; instead they receive judgment, attack, and often death. This happens when the majority of the Teacher's audience cannot relate to peaceful thinking. In contrast, their thinking is orientated toward judgment, conflict, and attack.

Socrates taught his pupils that the development of the mind through logic was the true path toward inner peace. He also taught that the pursuit of money and extravagance did not promote true happiness. The Greek aristocrats of the Senate accused him of corrupting the youth of Athens and forced him to drink poison.

Plato was a student of Socrates and an example that Socrates' teachings corrupted no one.

Yeshua (Jesus) followed the Socratic tradition and confounded his detractors with the Socratic method of answering questions with a more insightful question. His logic skillfully challenged tradition, and his peace teachings also threatened Roman militarism. Tacitus, a Roman historian, records the fact that Pilot ordered Jesus's crucifixion. The Bible myth describing Pilot as having no part in this murder is obviously not true. This manipulation of the facts is an attempt to cover up the Roman involvement in Jesus's death, and then three hundred years later, making him the head of the church. This is the reason the Bible falsely depicts the Jews as the sole perpetrators. This myth has led to a continuous chain of Jewish persecutions for a murder they had no legal power to commit.

Gandhi is another Peace Teacher who was assassinated because he was a living example that peace can be achieved without the use of hatred, guns, or armies. He defeated the imperial power of England by refusing to cooperate with tyranny.

Dr. King, John Kennedy, and Robert Kennedy were assassinated for peacefully asking that the constitutional rights of all citizens be available through equal justice under the law. They knew that partial justice is a contradiction in definitions.

This book is an attempt to diagnose the pathogens responsible for the disease of incivility; it also offers a logical cure.

Like all vaccines, it will only work for those who are willing to receive it. Everyone is offered the opportunity, but few choose to accept. This refusal to accept is the condition that results in the reoccurring epidemic of conflict and war.

There will come a day when all are immunized, and then the disease of conflict and attack will disappear. It will eventually become an offer that no one will choose to refuse.

TABLE OF CONTENT

THE TWO WOLF STORY

A long time ago on Turtle Island, a Native American grandfather was explaining the meaning of life to his grandson. He said, "Grandson, we are born with two wolves inside our mind that are fighting for our spirit. One wolf is mean, angry, and vengeful; the other wolf is kind, forgiving, and cooperative."

The grandson was alarmed and said, "But, Grandfather, which wolf is going to win?"

The grandfather smiled and said, "Whichever one you feed the most, Grandson; whichever one you feed the most."

The dynamics of this two-wolf story are currently being played out in modern society in the form of two diametrically opposed belief systems.

A) The Two Churches

There are two churches at work in the modern world: the Church of Truth and the church of the ego. One of them is true. The other merely believes it is true. One of them represents the Teachers of Peace; the other claims to represent the teachers of peace. Consequently, it is sometimes difficult to distinguish one from the other; therefore it may be helpful to examine the differences in their beliefs in order to see if this will help us decide which one appears to be the most able to point the way to True Peace.

The Church of Truth teaches that judgment and attack block the pathway to peace because no one has the right to impose their will on another human being; such impositions engender conflict, not peace.

The church of the ego, however, teaches the opposite. It believes that peace comes when evil is vanquished. It judges the world by an exclusive set of self-conceived concepts of what it considers to be good and evil and thereby believes that peace cannot be achieved until evil is attacked and vanquished. This method of separating the world into the good people and the bad people is a predictable process for creating a continuously unstable world devoid of peace.

This instability is best understood when we witness how concepts of good and bad are constantly changing; last decade's bad people are this decade's good people. Last decade's enemy becomes this decade's ally. Such inconsistencies are observable throughout human history, and this is the very inconsistency that guarantees the process of perpetual conflict.

War has its beginnings when someone believes attack is justified; the key word here is "believes." The introduction to this book describes how everything begins with a belief, or thought, before it manifests as a physical result. Therefore the examination of belief, or thought, will be the major focus of the remaining chapters of this book.

The world's belief in conflict is a self-fulfilling prophecy, and it is society's willingness to promote such a belief that assures its continued manifestation.

The next chapter will outline the basic process of misdirected or illogical thinking. Such thinking is obviously incapable of resolving conflict.

THE EGO AND THE ID

While Sigmund Freud was normalizing human homicide with his concept of the Id, Erich Fromm was contradicting Freud's theory by describing war as a pathology. Fromm concluded that homicidal behavior is abnormal.

Desmond Morris, a zoologist, agreed with Fromm when he said it is abnormal for like-species to kill like-species. Morris observed the mating rituals of animals and discovered that males only battle until one concedes that the opponent is stronger, and then the contest ends. Morris suggested that there is a survival mechanism in animal instinct that inhibits the killing of like-kind because the survival of the herd or pride depends on strength in numbers. If lions kill lions, the baboons will encroach on the territory of the weakened pride.

There are explainable anomalies to this mechanism. For instance, a mother rabbit, under stress, might eat her newborn young. This happens when environmental stress causes the mother rabbit to conclude that this is not the optimum time for raising her young. She then reabsorbs the nutrients in order to wait for a more advantageous time to raise a litter; this is a complicated survival mechanism.

A) Freud versus Fromm

Why did Freud become famous while Fromm faded into obscurity? The simplistic, but also valid, answer is that our social belief systems prefer to normalize the abnormal practice of homicidal war. A more complicated explanation is integrated into the Machiavellian philosophies that promote imperialism. (We will analyze this process later.)

B) Overcoming Instinct

This instinctual repulsion for participating in murder is the number one reason for military, boot-camp conditioning; recruits have to be desensitized to homicide. This desensitization process is inadequate for totally blotting out our natural instinct to avoid homicide. We can observe the failure of this conditioning by witnessing the high rate of posttraumatic stress disorder in combat veterans. The basic etiology for the occurrence of PTSD is the observation of, or participation in, the violent death of other human beings.

In our current series of wars in the Middle East and Gulf, the number of suicides associated with PTSD exceeds the number of combat deaths; a soldier's mind is more likely to kill him than an enemy bullet.

C) Ego Psychology

Freud is credited with opening a new window into the functions of the mind. He liberated us from the medieval concept of demon possession as a cause for mental illness, and he was a pioneer in pointing the way to modern mental-health treatment. Nevertheless, most of his theories for therapy have been rendered obsolete by advanced research and techniques.

Freud's daughter Anna continued in the family tradition and went on to develop the details of ego psychology.

By examining a few of these ego defense mechanisms, we can evaluate their usefulness for helping the mind stay in touch with logic and reality. We will only examine five of these mechanisms in order to see if we believe they are helpful.

Everyone has heard of the ego defense of denial—the ability of the mind to block out or slowly process undesirable or uncomfortable information. This is helpful when we suffer loss and the denial mechanism partially inhibits the mind's acceptance of reality, thus preventing the full trauma of the loss from overwhelming us. Under normal circumstances, this process fades as we slowly adjust to the reality of the loss.

Denial can lead to problems if it becomes a more permanent part of our mental functioning. This distortion of reality is common among individuals who develop continuous habits of alcohol or drug abuse. Understanding how this distortion develops is rather easy to observe. It begins with the shame and guilt messages associated with drug and alcohol abuse. Every time I hear someone say, "Your drinking is getting out of control," I call on denial to block the message. No one has taught me that this uncontrollable compulsion of addiction is linked to a genetic predisposition and that these constant shame and guilt messages actually drive me toward the ego defenses that will lead me further and further away from reality. The more often I hear, "Your drinking is so stupid" or "Can't you see how you are ruining your life?" or "If you loved me, you'd stop doing this," this constant stream of shame and guilt triggers the ego defense mechanisms, and I begin to lose touch with logic and reality. The ego has a whole menu of defenses that will help me escape the pain of shame and guilt.

Projection often becomes a favorite defense as the ego slowly takes over the addicted mind. We have all witnessed this process when someone says, "I wouldn't drink like this if my wife wasn't such a nag" or "I have to take drugs to cope with my lousy job" or "My childhood was so bad, I drink to deal with the pain." This process of projecting the blame onto others becomes a habit; the more I use it, the farther from reality I travel.

Minimizing is also a helpful cover-up. It's a close cousin to the denial defense. "You think my drinking is bad; I know people who drink twice as much as I do."

Rationalization fits well into this ego combo when I learn to say, "I only smoke pot; I don't do the hard stuff," or "Beer isn't harmful; it's those guys who drink scotch and vodka who have a real problem."

Over time this escape from reality deepens as the ego helps me block out the shame and guilt messages. A prime example of this process is found in nicotine addiction. There is a note on the side of the cigarette package that says, "These things can kill you." Yet how often do we hear denial and rationalization at work when someone says, "My grandpa smoked two packs a day, and he lived to be ninety." The truth is that nicotine addiction provides a stark reminder for understanding the meaning of the words "uncontrollable compulsion."

D) Fixing the Bad Wolf

In 1935 the recovery group known as Alcoholics Anonymous described the addiction process as a disease. But this disease does not follow a medical model. It is a composite problem of the "body, mind, and spirit." This definition takes it beyond a medical explanation.

The word body in this sequence is best understood in reference to a genetic predisposition, the DNA or gene connection. This DNA connection can be disclosed by examining the incidence of addiction in any of our extended family members. If one or more siblings, parents, grandparents, aunts, uncles, or cousins have an addiction problem, it is an indication that the genetic predisposition is transmitted in the family DNA.

When this problem is observed in a hereditary pattern, the best means for avoiding the problem is to never start it. In other words, I can live without drugs or alcohol. This concept of abstinence is based on the scientific principle found in epidemiology.

While scientists were describing the DNA sequence, other scientists began questioning the process. For instance, if I have a DNA marker for Alzheimer's disease, why doesn't it express when I am thirty years old? Or why does it wait until I am sixty-five to turn itself on? These kinds of questions led to the discovery that even though I have a DNA predisposition to a particular illness, but if I don't aggravate it with an environmental irritant, the DNA switch may not turn itself on. This explains why abstinence from alcohol can prevent the addiction switch from being activated.

A reference to the mind in our disease concept has already been discussed. When the ego defenses, or the Bad Wolf, take over the mind, a cloud of deception begins to blot out my ability to see the path back to reality.

I believe the spirit part of this body-mind-spirit concept is best understood by our previous story about the two wolves fighting for my spirit. When the ego defenses lead me farther and farther from reality, it's comparable to the Bad Wolf taking over my spirit. The process for fixing all three of these broken pieces is explained in the *Big Book of AA*. The individual case histories and the structure of the Twelve Steps are an effective guide for putting the Good Wolf back in charge.

There have been many attempts to invent a pharmacological cure for the addiction process, but this approach only addresses the body portion of this triad; it neglects to address the problem of the unhealed mind and spirit. I may stop putting alcohol or drugs into my body, but my mind and spirit are still controlled by that Bad Wolf. It becomes difficult under these circumstances to consider this to be an effective cure.

It's interesting how drug companies make money inventing pills that cause addiction and also make money selling pills that are supposed to fix the problem. If pills cause the problem, it is ironic to ask me to believe that pills can also fix it.

I have saved the discussion of the most interesting ego defense for last because I think it's the most difficult of the other four to normalize; it's called reaction formation. This defense suggests that I can have two opposing views in my mind and maintain mental balance. This is where the two-wolf story offers a practical way to evaluate this concept.

I think we can all agree that the reaction formation could be compared to the Bad Wolf and the Good Wolf being of equal strength, and therefore my life is balanced between good decisions and bad decisions. But how is this ambivalence supposed to help me? Or what do I feel like when I am not sure which voice to listen to? And does this really sound like something that can establish real stability in my life? I believe attempts to normalize this ambivalence are the root cause of our acceptance of the insanity of war. It's actually a Bad Wolf' trick to make me believe I can be happy with this ambivalence. The Bad Wolf knows that if I realize he's blocking my serenity, I might decide to stop feeding him. The possibility of me making such a decision strikes fear in the Bad Wolf's mind. Now he's no longer willing to be my friend.

In our next chapter, we will examine the structure and motivation for imperialism and see how the individual parts combine to produce a never-ending history of conflict.

HOW TO START A WAR

In AD 65 someone thought it would be helpful to add these words to the ending of the Gospel of Mark, "Go into all the world and preach the Gospel to every creature." Bible scholars know that these words were never in the original text. Nevertheless, this mistake became the beginning of the belief that Christians were supposed to evangelize the whole world.

By tracing a sequence of events from this error, it should become obvious that the misinterpretation or misallocation of these words not only fails to teach the original intentions of peacefulness but also results in the exact opposite.

On a sleepy Sunday morning in December 1941, the citizens of the United States were awakened from their slumber to hear President Roosevelt say, "A state of war exists between the United States and the Empire of Japan." He concluded with the iconic proclamation that, "This date shall live in infamy."

A traceable chain of events led up to this attack on Pearl Harbor, but the study of history in isolated pockets fails to demonstrate how the pieces of the chain are interconnected. This sequence of events extends over three hundred years and therefore is easily overlooked unless we know how to follow the tracts of the ego.

There is an interesting phenomenon in Chaos theory called the Butterfly Effect. It postulates that the turbulence generated by a butterfly flapping its wings in Brazil can express itself as a tornado in Kansas. Perhaps we can apply this Butterfly Effect to Japan's decision to bomb Pearl Harbor in 1941.

This sequence of events begins in AD 65 with a thought—the erroneous belief that Christians are supposed to evangelize the world.

In the latter half of the sixteenth century and the early half of the seventeenth century, Christian missionaries were hard at work spreading the Gospel in China and Japan. Dominicans from Spain, Jesuits from Portugal, and Protestants from England and Europe were busy at their task.

These ambassadors for peace began competing with one another in an effort to win converts to their particular brand of theology; this infighting was being observed by the host governments. The social turmoil generated by this Christian competition reached a crescendo when the missionaries began attacking Buddhism as promoting idol worship. (This is an interesting oversight by these missionaries since they had a variety of their own "idols.")

As a result of this social turmoil, the Japanese government, in 1638, put an end to this disturbance by expelling Christians from their country. This prohibition against European intrusion remained in place for over two hundred years.

The next link in this chain of events happened in 1765, with James Watt's perfection of the steam engine. This invention sparked the beginning of the Industrial Revolution.

Historians glamorize this revolution as a great leap forward for Western civilization; money and profits become the means for keeping score. Unfortunately, there is a new variable introduced by this rapid increase in mechanized production. Domestic markets could not absorb the extra production, and the necessity for opening foreign markets becomes obvious. The closed-door policies of China and Japan stood in the way of profits.

The next link materializes in 1854 when Commodore Perry, the American hero of the battle of Lake Erie, entered a Japanese harbor with ten steam-driven warships and forced the Japanese government to open trade with the West.

The Western merchants pounced on this opportunity, and by 1865 European and American allies imposed a formal treaty on the then-helpless government of Japan. It may be helpful at this point in the narrative to imagine the effects that these insults were having on the growing anger of the Samurai warriors.

Japanese officials were well informed concerning the industrialization of Europe and could see that circumstances dictated the necessity to adopt the new technology or continue to be the victims of abuse by the Western allies.

By 1899 Japan had industrialized to a level equal to the more advanced European powers, and well ahead of Russia. Japan was no longer willing to be the victim of Western imperialism.

While Japan was modernizing, the United States fought the Spanish American war and consequently took over the governance of Cuba, Porto Rico, and the Philippine Islands. Historians claim that the American government had intentions of granting independence to the Philippine Islands, but the delay of these intentions meant that the American government had permanent military instillations operating at the backdoor of Japan.

Simultaneous to this sequence of events, Western imperialism was imposing itself on the government of China. This resulted in the Boxer Rebellion of 1900, which was suppressed by the Western allies. At this same time, the English were encouraging the opium addiction of the Chinese people, similar to their strategy of using alcohol to subjugate Native Americans.

Japan was observing this Machiavellian abuse by the Western powers and could see that the volatility created by imperial greed had no boundaries or morals.

The insanity continued, and from 1898 to 1905, business interests in Europe and Russia were competing with each other to exploit Asia. This encroachment motivated Japan to attack and defeat the Russian army and navy in an attempt to prohibit the establishment of Western influence along the eastern coast of Russia and the coastline of the Sea of Japan. The Japanese were still chafing from the earlier abuses of the Western allies and decided to adopt the Western rules of smash and grab. They were proving to be fast learners.

In 1915 the Japanese were again reminded that Western greed was like a disease. They sat and watched as the allies turned on one another and Christians began murdering Christians by the millions in what historians were calling the war to end all wars. The First World War was fought by the same Christians who earlier attempted to evangelize China and Japan claiming they represented the Prince of Peace.

After this War to End All Wars reduced the cities of Europe to rubble, it took less than twenty years for inflamed egos to do it all over again in what Hollywood too often glamorizes as the Second World War.

The insanity of it all convinced the Japanese that an effective offence was their best defense, and they decided to attack all the military installations that threatened their island. Pearl Harbor contained the warships that supported all the US military bases in the Pacific Ocean that directly threatened the security of Japan.

The Butterfly Effect came to its conclusion at Pearl Harbor. This Butterfly Effect is related to the axiom that every action produces a reaction. A corollary to this rule suggests aggression is met with aggression. This simple logic seems to be lost in the volumes of words that are composed to cover up or cloud the obvious truth of this logic.

In the next chapter, we will consider some of the catch phrases that the ego uses to manipulate public opinion.

GODLESS COMMUNISM

When we hear the judgmental statement that someone or something is Godless, it should be a warning that we are hearing a sermon originating from the church of the ego.

When we ask the ego how a perfect God can create imperfect, Godless people, we are told that by free will they choose to be Godless. By this ego logic, we are forced to conclude that the Godless are more powerful than God. How else can the Godless override the will of God who desires that all of creation return to Him in eternity, which is everyone's natural inheritance?

The church of the ego depends on this process of separation through judgment. How else can the ego know whom to attack? The ego believes that when Yeshua said, "Judge not," he must have misunderstood the ego's need for separation and attack.

The church of the ego claims that Jesus is its Lord, but it also believes it has the power to disregard what its Lord says. This definitely sounds like an ego problem. Yeshua understood this ego confusion when he said, "Why do you call me Lord, but do not what I say?" (Luke 6:46).

14

A) More Butterflies

Millions of words have been recorded in thousands of history books in an attempt to piece together the various circumstances that culminated in the Russian revolution. This barrage of words is an ego trick and an attempt to use confusion in order to hide the easy-to-describe and predictable consequences of following the beliefs of the church of the ego.

When business men and politicians, who controlled the wealth of the Industrial Revolution, used their power and influence to exploit the working-class through the use of low wages, long and unreasonable work hours, and unsafe working conditions, they created the circumstances that would culminate in the Russian revolt.

This process is an understandable application of the principle of tension and release; inhuman treatment of the working-class created a buildup of tension, and the revolution was the release.

Greek philosophers understood this process when they described how a large and prosperous middle class modified the tension generated by an unsympathetic government dominated by self-centered aristocrats; the larger the middle class, the lower the tension level. Problems begin to develop when increasing dominance by the upper classes shrinks the size of the middle class and the original buffer against tension buildup is compromised. Eventually the release of tension is expressed by revolt.

The study of both Greek and Roman history demonstrates the reoccurrence of this easy-to-understand process.

Greek and Chinese philosophers also described the social cycles associated with this tension and release sequence, but the Chinese Dynastic Cycle is easier to articulate. It begins with a benevolent emperor coming to power, and his rule is just and the people are happy. Next he appoints a bureaucracy to administer the affairs of his expanding kingdom. Over time corruption begins to creep into the bureaucracy, and, as the corruption grows, tension begins to increase. The final part of the cycle takes place when the tension is released by revolt and a new benevolent emperor is installed. This process of tension and release has been the pattern for the rise and fall of governments for over ten thousand years.

B) Who Started the Cold War

At the beginning of the twentieth century, big business was in control of the governments of the West. This is why the governments were complicit in allowing the exploitation of the working class. Karl Marx, a scholar of the late nineteenth century, observed the development of this working-class abuse and wrote comments concerning the growing difference between the rich and the poor. The ego's use of projection and denial is illustrated by what happens next.

The egos that ran big business denied that they were abusing the working class, and they projected their guilt onto people like Marx. They denied their complicity by claiming that Marx's ideas inflamed the minds of the workers. This was an ego trick to divert attention away from the true cause of the tension.

When the Russian revolt began in 1917, big business and the governments they influenced were frightened by the Russian workers success. In response, these Western governments sent troops to invade Russia in an attempt to help the White Russians defeat the Bolsheviks and crush the revolution. Here again we see the beginning of the Butterfly Effect. Western powers invade Russia, but they are repulsed, and the revolution succeeds. This first attempt by Western governments to defeat the worker's revolt was accompanied by an additional and more callous message to the Russian working class. It came in 1921 when a severe drought resulted in the deaths of millions of Russian peasants. The same European powers, which tried to defeat the revolution by military intervention, now stood by and refused to send humanitarian aid to the starving peasants.

The Soviet leaders retaliated with a propaganda message urging all the workers of the world to revolt. Western governments and big business were obviously frightened by the political impact of this propaganda. The possibility of a workers' revolt was real; the observable success of the Russian peasants was tangible proof.

Each side in this ego struggle has its own version of the good guys and the bad guys. It is easy to discern how the ego is working both sides of the street in what comes to be known as the Cold War. The process of attack and counterattack is pure ego.

The next frightening piece in this drama comes eight years later with the stock-market crash of 1929. This economic failure added validity to the communist propaganda concerning big business and its control of government.

The hardships of the depression caused unemployed workers in America to consider the communist propaganda; this growth of communist appeal was cause for concern.

Four years after the stock-market crash, working-class Americans responded to the social-reform message of a Democratic candidate for the US presidency, and Franklin Roosevelt won by a landslide.

Under his leadership, laws regulating the previous economic recklessness that caused the depression were enacted. The Glass–Steagell Act prevented bankers from using bank funds for stock-market speculation; bankers were confined to the banking business, and economic speculators were confined to the stock and commodities markets, but the two processes could no longer be mixed. (Sixty years later this restriction will be undone.)

Social security, unemployment insurance, and workers' compensation laws were passed in order to provide a minimum of protection against abject poverty—the very poverty that led to the communist revolt.

Laws protecting workers' rights to form trade unions were enacted. The ability of the working class to negotiate reasonable wages and working conditions was the single most important step in preventing communism from gaining a foothold in America. When workers had the means for securing reasonable compensation from their employers, the necessity for revolt disappeared. (Fifty years later corporate control of government will erode these gains.)

Corporate fear of the communist message surfaced again in the 1950s when the intrusion of Western powers into Korea threatened China. The Chinese were familiar with the previous consequences of the Western invasion of their country in the late eighteenth and early nineteenth centuries. The economic motivation and political arrogance for these Western invasions had not disappeared, and the Chinese responded by helping North Korea push the Allied Armies out of North Korea and away from China's borders.

This scenario played itself out again ten years later when the French colonial presence in Vietnam was no longer tolerated. The Chinese were not willing to allow Western imperialism to threaten their borders.

With the defeat of France in Vietnam, political, economic, and religious forces within the United States spread false rumors concerning an alleged attack by communists at the Gulf of Tonkin. The "Red Scare" and "Godless Communism" propaganda by corporate-controlled media began shouting that if Vietnam went communist, all of Southeast Asia would follow.

America went to war in Vietnam because of these false rumors, and over fifty thousand American lives were sacrificed to the gods of the church of the ego and its propaganda.

Vietnam went communist, communism did not spread to Southeast Asia as predicted, and the Red Scare lost credibility. Just like the previous experience in Korea, the Chinese put a stop to repeated attempts to establish a Western military presence in their back yard. The millions of lives and billions of dollars wasted on this insanity can be directly related to the attack messages of the church of the ego.

When military officers in Vietnam reported the increased insubordination by draftees who refused to obey illegal or illogical orders, a decision was made to end the process of the draft. This decision was not the act of a benevolent or caring government; fear motivated the change. Drafting civilians who were no longer willing to follow unreasonable or illegal orders was a cause for concern in the minds of military and government leaders—leaders who depended on the blind loyalty of the troops they commanded. The divine right of kings began losing credibility.

Anyone born after 1975 may not be aware of how eighteen-year-old American males were subjected to the military draft. Military service was not voluntary as it is today. The lottery system was used to select those who would serve. Previous to 1975 there were minor objections to this process because it was not difficult to convince patriotic Americans that America's involvement in the First and Second World Wars was necessary. But this idea of necessity began to be questioned when our involvement in Korea was called a "police action," and there was no actual declaration of war by Congress because there was no direct attack by North Korea against the United States. This same questionable involvement resurfaced again in Vietnam. There was no true attack by Vietnam against the United States.

Concerned Americans were beginning to question the justification for our involvement in these police actions.

Lies about our reason for being in Vietnam, lies about combat casualties, and news report describing the massacre of Vietnam civilians ended any attempt by the government to justify the war. When riots broke out across the United States, politicians were no longer confident they could manipulate the American public. Grassroots protests ended the war, and the military draft was replaced by our current volunteer system.

When president and former army general Dwight Eisenhower was leaving office in 1961, he warned the American public that the growth of the "Military-Industrial Complex" was becoming a threat to American democracy.

The constitutional responsibility for declaring war is delegated to Congress in article 1, section 8, of the Constitution. The term "police action" not only subverts section 8 but also sets a precedent for ignoring Congress's involvement in the process. And when a handful of men in the executive branch of government are allowed to override the constitutional participation of Congress, we are headed toward a dictatorship. The obvious intention of section 8 is to delegate the serious responsibility for declaring war to debate and discussion by Congressmen, not a handful of people in a branch of the government that has no clear constitutional right to make such decisions. Section 8 also contains an additional reminder that Congress—not the president—is to have serious control of these decisions about war. Section 8, paragraph 12, clearly states that it is Congress that is responsible "to raise and support armies, but no appropriation of money to that use shall be for a longer term than TWO YEARS." Careful reading of the article reveals that a reserve army or militia is to be the primary protector of the nation. If every state in the union has a militia, an invasion by a foreign power would be met by the combined forces of every state in the union. The invaders would face more than ten million armed citizens. Even in today's military terms, this is a formidable force. (We will expand on this concept in a later chapter).

It appears that the composers of the Constitution and article 8 understood the dangerous effect that continuous war could have on the Treasury of the United States. The seriousness of this current subversion of the Constitution is demonstrated by viewing the composite bar graphs of the military budgets of all the major governments of the world. The US military budget exceeds half a trillion dollars annually and dwarfs the budgets of China, Russia, England, Germany, France, and so on. This subversion of Congress's responsibility to protect the US Treasury against the intrusion of the Military-Industrial Complex is the true reason millions of Americans have no health insurance. It is also the reason that the $3.2 trillion social security trust fund has been raided in order to finance these illegal wars—wars promoted by those who profit from subverting the Constitution. This is also the true reason the national debt continues to grow. War is expensive.

The United States has engaged in a series of unconstitutional "police actions" since the 1950s, and there is no indication that any branch of the US government is interested in curtailing these intrusions of the Military-Industrial Complex and its subversion of American democracy.

It appears that the bureaucratic corruption described in the Dynastic Cycle is growing bigger with the illegal and corrupt decisions to engage in these police actions.

C) The Fourth Branch of Government

We are taught in school that the US Constitution describes the duties of each of the three branches of government: the legislative, executive, and judicial.

The appearance of the fourth branch of government began several decades ago with what was then called the OSS. It was the part-time hobby of a few thrill-seeking rich kids who thought that the clandestine world of spying was excitingly romantic. (Check the net for William Donovan, Arthur Cannon Doyle, etc.)

This colorful hobby eventually grew into the more serious organizations that came to be known as the American CIA. and the British MI5 and 6. In the beginning they were assigned the legitimate responsibility for gathering and reporting information concerning the actions and intensions of foreign governments. This information was then passed on to the various government agencies responsible for formulating foreign policy, a quite orderly and necessary process of proper government.

All things seem to start with good intentions until the ego begins to take over. The spy people grew to resent the constitutional oversight of Congress and began devising ways to circumvent the system; a secret government within the government began to develop. The spies began overthrowing democratically elected governments that interfered with American business interests. They avoided Congressional oversight of their budgets and finances by trading drugs for guns; the guns that were necessary for conducting the secret and illegal wars they promoted. (See *The Agency*, by John Ranelagh, or the 1975 Church Committee investigations.)

Volumes have been published about the illegal and unconstitutional actions of the US intelligence agencies, but once the ego gets a foothold, it is difficult to reverse the process. Americans seem convinced that this is a method for maintaining our dominance in the world, and this method is also necessary for our continued access to foreign oil.

I saw a bumper sticker that said, "What's Our Oil Doing under Their Soil?" What a poetic way for the ego to express its acceptance of the idea that "might make right." But all this delusional thinking merely reveals how the ego clouds reality. There are no true reasons we need to steal other people's oil. The countries that are big oil producers are also in semidesert locations. Their agricultural ability to produce all their own food is limited. They can't withhold their oil; they, by necessity, need to sell their oil in order to survive.

Big-business propaganda has invented the idea that if America doesn't protect the oil fields then Americans won't have gasoline for their cars. This fear message is all that is necessary in order to fool gullible Americans into believing the hoax.

It is true that the smaller countries that produce oil need protection from all sorts of unscrupulous people. But American protection is a cover story. US corporations, with the help of the CIA., set up dictatorships in these countries. These dictators agree to cooperate with the exploitation of their country's natural resources, and the dictators benefit quite handsomely, but the general population does not.

This intrusion and exploitation by American corporations is the major cause for the turmoil we currently see in the Middle East and Gulf regions. American troops are dying in order to protect major corporate profits—profits that should rightfully be used to benefit the citizens whose oil is being exploited.

Our government pretends to support and promote democracy, but nothing in the government's actions demonstrates this intention.

As corporations manipulate and subvert American democracy, how can we believe that they have any interest in promoting democracy elsewhere? The will of the people is of little or no importance to big business.

This duplicity does not go unnoticed by the Arab people.

The study of history has no value if the intrusions of the ego are normalized or glamorized while truth is avoided or ignored.

Every action invokes a reaction. Aggression is met with aggression. And exploitation is met with resentment and retaliation. This simple logic is lost in the volumes of words that are composed to cover up or cloud the truth of this logic.

In the next chapter, we will examine some of the mechanisms that help the ego obscure reality and set in motion the circumstances that lead to conflict.

THOU SHALL NOT STEAL

I t's interesting how we can teach the concept of evolution and simultaneously ignore the ecological processes associated with this biological sequence.

For instance, if extra rainfall increases grass production, and extra grass production increases rabbit fertility, and extra rabbit fertility increases fox fertility, there comes a point in this sequence where the trend reverses itself. Extra foxes eat extra rabbits, and fewer rabbits cause a decline in fox fertility, and nature reaches an equilibrium. This biological balance has been understood for decades because research validates the logic of this interdependence.

If these cycles of nature are not artificially disturbed by misuse, the ratio of sustainable human population in relation to the natural production of the soil assumes a balance related to the illustration of the foxes and the rabbits.

Thom Hartman in his book *The Last Hours of Ancient Sunlight* gives us a logically brilliant explanation as to how the industrial revolution continues to disrupt thousands of years of ecological balance.

Here again, the process is logical. For illustration purposes let's suppose that in its natural state, a hundred acres of land can produce enough food to feed thirty people. Our hunter-gatherer relatives maintained this natural state for thousands of years.

But the curious creature known as *Homo saipan* discovered that tilling the soil could increase food production. This new discovery increased the output of our theoretical hundred acres, and now it is able to feed sixty people. This change introduces a variable into our fox and rabbit story; human fertility is being increased by this "artificial" food production.

By the time we progress to the industrial revolution, our advancements in machinery, mining, and agriculture contribute to a population explosion. Nature sometimes intervenes with plagues, famines, or other natural disasters, but this is only a delaying mechanism; it doesn't curtail the overall fertility created by the corresponding increase in artificial food production.

An example of this unsustainable population is observed within the history of the seventeenth-century migration of Europeans to the Americas. European cities were desperately overcrowded. Territorial wars were a continuous result of this overpopulation. The religious and political prohibitions against birth control were a contributing factor to this turmoil.

Conditions in the Americas were the opposite. Populations were in harmony with the environment. Herbal medicines were available for either suppressing or enhancing fertility. The decision to have children was determined by an intelligent choice made by the parents and was unrelated to any external religious or political dogma.

Ecological sustainability has become a topic for modern scientific inquiry. Paul Ulrich in his book *Population Explosion* explains how water use by deep-well irrigation coupled with natural soil erosion is depleting these two most important components of food production. In other words, there is a limit or point of decline where these resources will fail to meet demand.

Earth's population currently exceeds seven billion people. Computer models suggest that an ecologically sustainable population for the Earth is approximately three billion. Food production is not the only variable in this calculation. Consideration for water and air pollution associated with human activity is included. The finite nature of mineral resources introduces its own limit. A historical example of this limit to natural resources can be seen with the history of Cyprus during the growth of the Greek city-states.

Cyprus had an abundance of mineral resources, and the island was covered with magnificent forests; commerce was booming. The lumber trade for shipbuilding was at its peak. Wood for smelting the mineral wealth was plentiful. But simple arithmetic could foretell that this boom would have a bust. The minerals became exhausted, the forests disappeared, and erosion removed the soil. Rocks became the only reminder of what was once a beautiful, tree-covered island.

Were the Greeks aware of the potential exhaustion of these resources? Of course they were. They were also aware that there were other lands to conquer and other resources to exploit. If a nation depletes its resources in one of its colonies, it can always go to war with the neighbors and acquire theirs. This has always been the motivation for war and imperialism.

Governments claim they desire world peace, but they ignore the true cause for their habitual cycles of exploitation. No one wants to acknowledge that excess population is the core catalyst for this problem. Religious, political, and commercial beliefs choose to ignore reality. This is why we call it the church of the ego; denial of reality is one of its prominent doctrines.

A) Go Forth and Subdue the Earth

There are several incentives for having lots of babies. In agricultural societies, large families are a source of labor. In imperial societies, lots of babies provide a constant supply of soldiers. If we don't have a superior army, how will we be able to acquire the neighbor's resources when the misuse of our own causes shortages? The love of luxury is a difficult addiction to overcome.

It's interesting to read how writers glorify the histories of Greece and Rome. They seem to gloss over the brutality, exploitation, and larceny of the ancestors of our current thinking processes. The exploits of war heroes and the triumphs of brutal rulers are glorified while the philosophers and peace advocates are curious incidentals. We claim to admire the logic of Socrates and Pythagoras and their modern examples like Kant and Spinoza, but we ignore the fact that their logic led them to reject the belief that money and extravagance are the source of happiness. They also had comments concerning the consequences of uncontrolled fertility, greed, and injustice. The ego is expert at creating blind spots in our perception. It rejects or ignores any logic that might expose its deceptions.

It's interesting to read how ruling classes in Greece and Rome became alarmed when the size of families began to decline. This decline was the natural result of farmers moving to the cities for increased opportunities, and simultaneously their need for larger families was no longer necessary. The aristocrats and generals were alarmed at this decline in potential cannon fodder for their imperial exploits. All manner of legal and religious coercion was employed in an effort to increase population. The irony in these histories is revealed when at various times and locations, the population exceeded the available food supply. Nevertheless, women were expected to produce soldiers for the empire. Women were socially ostracized when, for no fault of their own, they were unable to conceive. This focus on reproduction has persisted to our current time in history.

I have often thought that the biblical animosity toward homo-sexuality began with the ancient belief that the defense of the tribe was dependent on superior numbers. Consequently, anyone who didn't produce children was a threat to the survival of the community. It's the same core reason that, even in the face of modern conditions of overpopulation, objections to birth control persist. It's difficult to erase ancient fears even when they are no longer valid.

If the reader believes that abortion is the true reason for at-tacking family-planning clinics, I suggest reading the life story of Margret Sanger, the founder of Planned Parenthood, and learn firsthand what the controversy is truly about.

If you are angered by politicians, who believe they have the right to interfere with your personal choice to access birth control, then don't spend your vacation money in states that elect them.

B) Let's Not Talk about It

If scientific research shows us that the Earth is exceeding its abil-ity to maintain a sustainable increase in population, why is no one interested?

If I ask the business community to fund a grant for studying the negative effects of unsustainable population growth, will they be willing to finance the research? Their interests are obviously pointed in the opposite direction. Profits are directly linked to expanding markets, and expanding markets are related to popula-tion growth. Business and commercial enterprises are not inter-ested in sustainable population development.

If I turn to religion and make an appeal of compassion for the children who are born into societies that cannot feed or care for them, what am I told? The repeated excuse is that statistics sug-gest that there is plenty of food, and the real problem is poor dis-tribution. There are several obvious flaws with this excuse. Food production and availability are interdependent with a variety of economic and ecological factors. Suggesting that food distribution is the only problem is an illogical attempt to deflect attention away from the obvious need for population planning. Any organization (be it religious, political, or commercial) that thinks its interest are protected by larger numbers of believers is never interested in considering anything, no matter how logical, that interferes with its perceived need for increased fertility.

As of this writing the calculated cost for adequately raising a child from birth to age eighteen is approximately $220,000. Under these circumstances, can a single mom with three children and an annual income of $30,000 offer her children an equal opportunity to compete on the playing field of life?

Suggesting that food distribution is the only problem offers no real solution; it's an excuse to ignore the true problem.

If I appeal to the government to engage in the process of population planning; what should I expect?

Governments run on taxes, and taxes are paid by people. Increased population results in increased revenue. Under these circumstances, there is no incentive for governments to deliberately engage in the encouragement of family planning.

Since antiquity governments have encouraged population growth in order to develop military strength. This concept of strength in numbers is an unconscious belief predating the Stone Age. And, although this archaic belief has been rendered obsolete by technology, it is still an artifact in the primitive mind.

The religious and political resistance to population planning can be seen in the vehement criticisms of the Chinese government's decision to take an active role in family planning. Chinese leaders based this decision on the logic that continuous, uncontrolled population growth was leading the country toward catastrophic social consequences. External interests chose to ignore this logic, which then resulted in repeated attacks by foreign religious and political organizations. This willingness to deny reality is an indication that the church of the ego was involved.

C) What Are the Consequences

John Calhoun did an interesting experiment in order to illustrate the consequences of uncontrolled population growth. (See "mouse utopia" on the net.) He placed pairs of mice in a box and provided them with all the material resources that mice need for survival, with the exception of unlimited space; the walls of the box defined the environment.

In the beginning the mice did what mice normally do. They formed pairs, built nests, and raised babies. Mothers fed their babies, and fathers helped gather food. As time passed, the babies grew up to form families of their own, and the population of the box grew exponentially. Food and material were in constant supply but space was limited.

As the box became overcrowded with mice, social instincts began to deteriorate. Fights broke out due to territorial disputes. Pair bonds loosened, and some mothers were not as focused on childcare as they previously were. And some mice solved their stress by crawling into a corner and dying. The social norms of the mouse community deteriorated as the population increased.

There are other studies that illustrate similar consequences of overcrowding. Experimenters found that testosterone levels in males became elevated in direct relation to population density associated with inner-city living conditions. These elevated testosterone levels suggest a correlation between overcrowding and increased incidence of aggression and violence.

Our previous description of the tension and release principle seems to be evident in this condition. This also gives us an opportunity to illustrate the difference between the Good Wolf's and the Bad Wolf's thinking. The Good Wolf would suggest exercise, sports, and intimacy as positive choices for tension release. City-planners understand this principle when they make space for parks and playgrounds where sports and exercise offer nonviolent opportunities for tension release.

In contrast, the Bad Wolf likes aggression, physical violence, and rape as means for releasing tension. This is why city planners budget for police departments and jails.

Military recruiters rely on this testosterone principle as a mean for enlisting eighteen-year-old males. Older, more mature males are not as vulnerable to the limited experience that hinders the thinking processes of eighteen-year-olds.

Future research will demonstrate how environmental stressors produce negative effects on a woman's body chemistry during gestation and, consequently, create a variety of insults to the development of the fetus.

When humans choose to ignore the stressors of overpopulation, nature intervenes.

In our next chapter, we will examine the various ego defenses that help maintain the belief systems of religion, science, and commerce and encourage them to ignore the research that supports the social advantages associated with family planning and population management.

HOW THE EGO MAKES
EXCUSES

As evidence increases to verify the wisdom of population planning, it becomes increasingly necessary for certain belief systems to manufacture excuses for ignoring reality. In a previous chapter, we discussed how the ego offers us many mechanisms for blotting out or ignoring facts. The following are a few of the more obvious illusions fabricated by the ego process.

Certain branches of science provide us with research to verify our need for population planning. Ecologists have supplied us with an abundance of evidence demonstrating our need to implement a plan for maintaining a sustainable balance between natural resources and human consumption, but there are other scientific opinions that can be used to minimize or rationalize disinterest in this ecological evidence. This is the erroneous belief that by the time we exhaust Earth's resources, we will have colonized other planets. This fantasy takes us back to the Greek solution for ignoring the limits of resources on the island of Cyprus, use them all up, and when they are gone, just move onto the next exploitable territory. *Star Wars* made a lot of money for Hollywood, but attempts to turn illusion into reality is a good definition for insanity.

The human body isn't designed for long-term space travel. It can barely survive travel within the confines of our own solar system, and before earth bodies figure out how to tolerate a trip to Alpha Centauri, the effects of ignoring the ecological degradation of Planet Earth will have destroyed any such endeavors.

There is information I have read that illustrates the futility of believing we can ignore the consequences of degrading our environment. Before the end of the twenty-first century, we will uncover artifacts on Mars that will reveal how the environment on that planet deteriorated and some of its inhabitants migrated to Earth. It is possible that DNA in these artifacts will substantiate this migration. If this sounds implausible, it may be helpful to review the current research conducted on Neanderthal remains and how it confirms the intermarriage of Neanderthals with *Homo sapiens.* It is also interesting that the cranial capacity of Neanderthals is larger than that of *Homo sapiens.* It's embarrassing to discover that last decade's "cavemen" are the source for this decade's larger brains for *Homo erectus.*

Our next example of ego denial is the religious belief that there is no need for the "good people" to be concerned with the future of Earth's ecology; they are all going to be raptured into the clouds before the bad stuff happens. This current popular myth is only a few decades old. A series of theological mistakes made it necessary to invent the story.

Early Christians failed to listen when Yeshua said, "My Kingdom is not of this world" because this statement conflicted with their belief in the scriptures that said the son of David would establish an earthly kingdom. This wish for an earthly kingdom also ignored Yeshua's reminder that "God is Spirit and is worshipped in spirit." These statements concerning a nonphysical, or Spiritual Kingdom, fell on deaf ears.

The next problem in this misunderstanding occurred when the rumor circulated that this earthly kingdom was about to happen. This wishful thinking may have resulted from the belief that God was about to help the Jews expel the Romans from Jerusalem.

None of these erroneous predictions materialized, and the revolt of the Jews in AD 70 resulted in the total destruction of Jerusalem.

With all these previous predictions up in smoke, it became necessary to revise the story. In AD 96 the *Book of the Revelation* proceeded to reinterpret the entire narrative in a psychedelic attempt to excuse the earlier errors. What was expected to be the establishment of an immediate kingdom was now projected into a future time.

There is a place in the *Revelation*, chapter 4, where the scripture describes a door open in heaven and a voice like a trumpet saying, "Come up here." This is where theologians claim that the rapture takes place. They couple this scripture with I Thessalonians 4 where we also hear a trumpet calling both the dead and the living "to be caught up in the clouds to meet the Lord in the air," and "so shall we be with the Lord forever."

Now, if this myth of the rapture concluded with these two references, it would be possible to make it sound logical. However, we have a problem. The scriptures that place us "forever with the Lord in heaven" reverse the process and send us back to Earth to help set up that earthly kingdom that we found out earlier wasn't supposed to be earthly. This confusing contradiction is necessary to explain how the people, who were born before they had a chance to believe in Jesus, were going to be preached to and given a chance to be baptized—or consequently get thrown into a burning hell. But now we've added more confusion because a burning hell is a Greek/Roman myth that has no legitimate place in Christian theology.

These repeated attempts to cling to the myths concerning an earthly kingdom were the product of limited information. These ancient authors had no true comprehension of how these myths would be undone by modern science.

The earth has no possibility of becoming a kingdom or earthly paradise. Our Sun will eventually become a supernova and consume all the planets, including Earth.

In addition to this material catastrophe, the whole universe will eventually disappear as every star in the cosmos burns out.

This is how we come full circle back to the insightful wisdom of Yeshua who told us His Kingdom is not of this world.

When religious myths remove or prevent us from a connection with reality, they also help the ego deny the need for logical solutions.

The scriptures also contain another contradiction that demonstrates the theological inability to accept a clear separation between material bodies and eternal spirit. We witness this confusion every time we attend a funeral.

Grieving friends and family members gather at church to bid farewell to a loved one who has died. The preacher begins his sermon by referring to Second Corinthians 5 where we are told, "To be absent from the body is to be present with the Lord." This is a comforting message for all those who are grieving the loss of a friend. The ability to imagine their loved one safe in Heaven residing with a benevolent Creator is the most appropriate message that could be delivered to this grieving audience.

If we could end the ceremony with this comforting message, it would be most appropriate, but now we caravan to the cemetery where the casket containing the body of the deceased is placed above a six-foot hole in the ground. The preacher then opens his Bible to Thessalonians where we are told that our loved one's body is going to wait there in the cemetery until that trumpet is blown and all the bodies in the cemetery are going to come up out of the ground to make a second trip up to Heaven.

I remember several decades ago seeing the illogical duplicity in these obviously conflicting stories. It would require an additional fifty years of study to discover which of these contradictions was the truth and which one was the product of Greek myth.

If the reader is interested in understanding this truth, the solution will be offered in the remaining chapters of this book.

The third and final group in this triad of ego-directed institutions is the global network of commercial and business organizations. These people believe they are realistic. They aren't fooled by religious myths. They are pragmatic; if it isn't physically tangible, it is obviously not real.

These are practical people who know that human lifespans rarely exceed a hundred years. All this talk about global warming, ecological degradation, and resource depletion is easy to ignore. These leaders of commerce and industry don't expect to live long enough to be effected by the consequences of their unbridled exploitation of the environment. They believe they will be dead and thereby escape the turmoil of their greed.

Believing that death is the end of life does not make it so. This false reliance on death as a final solution follows the characteristics of the ego defenses of both denial and rationalization. Our previous model concerning addiction and its need for the employment of the ego defenses to escape reality can now be expanded to other kinds of addiction. These captains of industry can be addicted to power, control, and money, along with a long list of other sentient-related escapes from reality.

In our next chapter, we will examine the expanded principle of "Reaping what we sow." If the pragmatic leaders of commerce and industry fully understood the implications of this truth, they might reconsider the belief that they can escape the consequences of their behavior.

THE AMERICAN BUDDHA

S everal hundred years before Europeans set foot on the shores of the Americas, there was a Native American who lived near the confluence of the Missouri and Mississippi Rivers. He was like the Buddha or Enlightened Teacher. The wisdom of his teachings spread far and wide and continues to be an important part of many traditional Native American philosophies.

A) The Star Trail

The original teaching of the Star Trail story should begin with an explanation concerning our "Earth Suits"; this is what I wear when my spirit is attending the Earth School. This Earth Suit, or body, is the vehicle for assisting the spirit in its journey or learning experiences. The body doesn't learn, but the mind or spirit does.

It's an observable fact that our Earth Suit wears out. When this happens, the spirit vacates the body and travels across the Star Trail (the Milky Way).

At the end of the Star Trail sits an Old Woman. She will ask me questions to determine if I have learned all the ways of a natural human being. If I give all the correct answers, I pass on into the Paradise. If I haven't learned all the ways of a natural human being, logic says that entering Paradise with uncorrected mistakes would interfere with the concept of Paradise.

If I can't answer all the questions, I am tossed off the Star Trail to drift back to the Earth School to acquire a new Earth Suit in order to continue my education. A loving Creator has arranged for everyone to have as many Earth School experiences as necessary. Everyone eventually enters Paradise because we all eventually learn the ways of a natural human being.

The language of this Star Trail metaphor may be Native American, but the same concept has been taught for centuries by every culture on this planet, including early Christianity.

Using the search words "transmigration of the soul" or "reincarnation" on the Internet or in history books can provide an abundance of information explaining the beginnings of this understanding in India and Greece, and how the teachings were carried to the four corners of the known world through commerce and trade on both land and sea.

The enlightenment of the Buddha began in India. Then it grew in China and Japan and is currently known or practiced in many other countries, including America.

The most interesting explanation for this concept of serial rebirth can be found in the logical comments of certain Greek philosophers such as Pythagoras, Parmenides, and Socrates. Their logic concluded that it was an observable fact that the minds of the philosophers were more advanced than those of the common people. But they reasoned that a Universal Mind or Source had, by the concept of perfection, the necessity to be just and thereby treat all beings equally. This school of philosophy then concluded that justice and equality for every mind required many life times of refinement; the untrained mind needed many opportunities to learn this perfection. Thus the concept of the transmigration of the soul emerged from this logical thought and was unrelated to religious mythology. This philosophical logic was also present in the seventeenth- and eighteenth-century comments of people like Kant, Spinoza, and Mendelssohn.

B) The Bible and Serial Rebirth

Between AD 326 and 553, when Christian theology was being transformed into a state religion, there was a concerted effort to remove all references to transmigration of the soul found in the early Christian writings. Fortunately, it wasn't possible to remove every reference from the accounts that were later organized into what we now call the Bible.

For instance, *Malachi*, the very last book of the Old Testament, tells us that Elijah will appear to announce the coming of the Messiah. This prophecy was written several hundred years after Elijah had died. Consequently, for Elijah to reappear, he would have to reincarnate. This is not an insignificant prophecy because it continues to be an important part of a contemporary, Jewish ceremony.

Every springtime at the Jewish celebration of Passover, there is a ritual meal called the Ceder. There is an empty plate placed at the end of the table and at a certain point in the recitation, Elijah is invited to join the meal. Logic tells us that Elijah cannot accept the invitation unless he reincarnates.

If we follow this significant prophecy on into the New Testament, it appears at Luke 1:17 where the father of John the Baptist is being told that his wife is going to give birth to a son, and this son will be called John, and "he will have the spirit and power of Elijah." This reincarnation story continues to resurface at Matthew 11:14 where Jesus tells his followers, "John the Baptist is Elijah, if you are willing to accept it." The next scripture that expands this concept of transmigration of the soul is found at Matthew 16:13 where Jesus asks his students, "Who do the people say I am?" The students respond by saying, "Some say John the Baptist, but others Elijah, and still others Jeremiah or one of the other prophets." These comments tell us that the belief in reincarnation is widespread in the community; how else can Jesus be considered the possible reappearance of so many former prophets? (John the Baptist had died before Jesus asked this question.)

I have discussed these scriptures with individuals who resist the concept of transmigration of the soul; they often say, "John is only a metaphor for Elijah, he wasn't a reincarnation." In response, I ask them to read Matthew 17, which summarizes the meaning of all these other scriptures.

This chapter in Matthew is referred to as the Transfiguration. Jesus takes some of his students up onto a mountain where He is transfigured into a Being of Light. His students were obviously frightened by the experience. In this enlightened state, Jesus had a conversation with Moses and Elijah in the other dimension.

Coming down the mountain, the students were confused. They said that the scribes teach that Elijah has to appear first before the Messiah arrives. Then they asked, "How can Elijah be in the other dimension if he is supposed to be here to announce your arrival?" Jesus answered them by saying, "He was here and they did to him what they are going to do to me." Then the scripture says that the students understood that Jesus was referring to John the Baptist; John was a reincarnation of Elijah, not a metaphor.

There is an apparent anomaly to this story at John 1:21 where the Levites ask John if he is Elijah and he says he isn't. How then do we explain this discrepancy? The short answer is how many reincarnations are remembered by anyone who is asked this question? The longer explanation can be understood by reading *Journey of Souls* by Dr. Michael Newton.

C) The Gospel of Thomas

Our references to passages in the Bible illustrating the concept of serial rebirth are not the only source of Christian commentary concerning this interesting subject. The reappearance of the Gospel of Thomas in 1948 at Nag Hammadi in Egypt helps us appreciate the scripture that tells us, "All things hidden will be revealed."

Theological efforts to suppress or hide the contents of the Sayings Gospels have been circumvented. Previous attempts to remove these Gospels became necessary because they contradicted the theology that entered the Cannon in AD 326.

The Gospels that were selected for inclusion in today's Bible were not directly related to any of their writers having face-to-face conversations with Jesus. These Gospels began as oral stories and weren't reduced to writing until decades after Jesus's transition.

The Gospel of Thomas, unlike these oral stories, records face-to-face conversations with Jesus. None of the Gospels in the Bible can make such a claim. (Only 70 of the 114 sayings in the Gospel of Thomas are original. A source for verifying this information will be given in suggested readings.)

There are several sayings in the Gospel of Thomas that are best understood through the concept of serial rebirth, but saying 84 is easily understood: "Yeshua said, 'When you see your likeness you are happy. But when you see your images that came into being before you and neither die nor become visible, what grandeur!'"

D) The Christian Priest Origen (AD 185)

The chronology of the Christian acceptance or rejection of the concept of transmigration of the soul takes place before and after AD 400. Writings previous to that date reflect a long history of preserving the acceptance. After that date the intensity of attempts to purge this concept from Christian theology become palpable, and by AD 553, they become severe.

A very well read and widely published Christian priest named Origen (Origenes Adamantius) understood and taught the transmigration of the soul. He appreciated the logic of those previous Greek scholars who reasoned that humans required several lifetime experiences in order for their minds to achieve maturity.

Although Greek Philosophers chose to refrain from giving a specific name to the Prime Source, they reasoned that the Source was perfect and pure and therefore extended justice to everyone and everything equally. The philosophers concluded that this concept of equal justice could only be accomplished if the soul had many life experiences in order to reach enlightenment.

There were scholars like Origen who saw these attributes as being totally compatible with the loving God described in the New Testament. There were others who eventually saw it as a contradiction to the new theology that was forming around the growing need for a state religion to unify the empire.

E) Today's Hero, Tomorrow's Heretic

Origen's career was maturing by the year AD 225, and he died approximately thirty years later. He was a prolific writer and a respected Christian priest and scholar.

By AD 325 the Roman Emperor Constantine had a vision of uniting the Roman Empire by making Christianity the universal state religion. He was present at the First Council of Nicaea where heads of the various Christian congregations assembled to debate the doctrines that would be accepted into or rejected from the official theology of this universal state religion. These debates were often hostile and sometimes violent; the pattern was set at this council for the habit of Christianity's failure to always be Christian.

The edicts of this council and its desire to formulate a unified doctrine set the tone for the heresy trials that would stain the pages of Christian history for the next thousand years.

By AD 400 the growing influence of the councils increased their motivation for purging the doctrine of any previous teachings contradicting the new theology. This caused the widespread teaching of the transmigration of the soul to be condemned. The original logic of a loving God allowing the spirit or soul many lifetimes to reach perfection or enlightenment came in direct conflict with the new doctrine of a burning hell and only one chance to obey the church. This concept of a burning hell was grafted into Christian theology from Greek and Roman mythology. There is no mention of a burning hell in the Old Testament. But as the New Testament was assembled, this Greek/Roman influence surfaces in the narrative and becomes incorporated into the doctrine.

Even though Bible scholars know that the hell-fire myth has no legitimate place in modern Christian theology, there are those who attempt to justify retaining the myth as being helpful for deterring crime.

Modern mental-health research disproves any notion that a steady diet of fear, shame, and guilt is an effective means for shaping positive social behavior. When these messages are used to "convict people of sin," they become problematic. As an example, is it sinful for a woman to walk down the street in New York City topless? But does this judgment lose meaning if we are in a tribal community in Africa, South America, or on the beach in the South of France? These contrasts in social norms should remind us why judgment is best left to local custom and should not be converted into a myopic, universal orthodoxy.

It's helpful to recall the logic of our previous axiom that says, "I do not respond well when someone tries to impose their will on me; why then do I believe I have the right to impose my will on those around me?"

There is a line in an Irish ballad that expresses the arrogance of believing we have the right to impose our personal beliefs on others; the poet expressed it perfectly when he said, "The strangers came and tried to teach us their ways, and they blamed us just for being who we are."

Illogical shame and guilt messages are often the root cause of a clinical condition called "self-sabotage." This occurs when my unconscious mind is convinced I am guilty and I believe that guilty people need to be punished. Confusion sets in when my unconscious need to be punished conflicts with what should be my conscious self-interest. This is why we chuckle at the story on the evening news about a bank robber who writes his stick-up note on the back of a deposit slip containing his name and address. This is not a mistake. It is self-sabotage, and criminologists and police detectives are well aware of this phenomenon.

I have witnessed otherwise intelligent people subvert their own self-interest by this process of self-sabotage. The problem is endemic to individuals who have been taught guilt messages that conflict with the normal processes of logical, human behavior. The problem starts with distorted thinking before it manifests as self-destructive behavior. Being selective about what goes into my mind determines my future.

Continuing to value the hell-fire myth as a useful means for maintaining social order is not only problematic but it also diverts our attention away from a process that is logically more effective.

The reality of serial rebirth is obviously a better incentive for moral behavior. The thought of repeatedly returning to the uncertainties of existence on Earth is enough motivation for any thinking person to learn to be a natural human being. I experienced the effectiveness of this process when I was using the Native American Medicine Wheel to illustrate the natural design of serial rebirth. At the end of the presentation, I asked the audience, by a show of hands, how many wanted to return to another incarnation? An audible groan went up from the audience, and people didn't raise their hand.

It appears by this audience reaction that learning to "treat others the way I want to be treated" takes on a greater significance when it is associated with serial rebirth. This may also be helpful for explaining the politeness I have experienced when associating with people who follow the peaceful traditions of the Buddha.

This is also an appropriate place to examine the extended meaning of "We reap what we sow" in the context of serial rebirth. This is especially helpful for reminding business leaders who believe they won't live long enough to experience the repercussions of their impact on the ecology. Their potential reincarnation into an environment, degraded by their previous lack of concern, takes on a new dimension of reality. Those who are enjoying a life of luxury today may find themselves reincarnating as a subsistence farmer in Bangladesh. This is also how "treating others the way we want to be treated" extends itself beyond our current time or place.

Another interesting learning experience occurs when a sexually abusive male reincarnates as a female or the self-righteous male, who believes he is doing God's work by blocking women's access to birth control, returns as a woman who has five children she struggles to feed.

Imagine how this process of serial rebirth eventually replaces callousness with compassion. It may take some individuals a thousand years of experiences, but everyone eventually learns how to "treat others the way they want to be treated."

Saying, "But for the grace of God there goes I," is replaced with, "When I offer grace, I receive grace." Just imagine the impact this new way of thinking will have on altering abusive behavior. Everyone will eventually learn it because we keep repeating the lessons until we get it perfect. This is the true meaning of "be perfect as your Heavenly Father is perfect" (Matt. 5:48). We get as many lessons as we need, even if it takes ten thousand years. We all eventually win because a loving God rejects no one.

F) The Other Dimension

Over a hundred years ago, a Native American mystic named Black Elk had a vision; today this would be referred to as a near-death experience. He went into the other dimension and had conversations with the Wisdom Teachers there. (Details are in the book *Black Elk Speaks*). His comments about what he learned are summed up in his description of what he witnessed: "This world is only a shadow of the Real World."

Gaining wisdom from these kinds of experiences is an integral part of Native American medicine.

In 1998 I was with a group in the outback of Peru. Our guide took us to a place at the base of a small mountain where we were introduced to a three-by-five-foot niche carved into the rock at the base of the mountain. The guide explained that the native medicine people kneel in that niche and pray themselves into the other dimension. This is how they receive information about the herbal medicines and other healing practices. I remember thinking how difficult it would be for a person, tutored in modern scientific theory, to accept such a story.

There is a paradoxical irony in this conflict of cultures when we learn that pharmaceutical companies send representatives into remote South American villages to obtain information from these herbal medicine people. The representatives ignore the indigenous person's explanation of how the information was received, but they have no problem using the information to make profits for their employers. I have been told that a group of indigenous medicine people have filed a lawsuit against a pharmaceutical company for proprietary infringement. It appears that perceiving indigenous people as ignorant, superstitious, savages is a misperception that is about to collide with twenty-first century indigenous enlightenment.

G) NDE

Near death experiences are an integral part of human history; every culture, both ancient and modern, has recorded these stories. Fear-based religions tend to avoid discussing these reports because the descriptions of the other dimension are so beautiful and serene they contradict the religious myths concerning a burning hell. (There are rare instances where individuals claim to have had a "hell" experience. Explanations as to how the mind can perceive such things are accessible in suggested readings.)

Two meaningful stories concerning the hell-fire myth are discussed in the following near-death experiences. In the book *The Light Beyond,* by Dr. Raymond Moody, there is an account describing the experience of one of these hell-fire preachers.

I paraphrase: when the hell-fire preacher vacated his body and went into the other dimension, he was greeted by a Being of Light who told the preacher that his hell-fire stories were making the people of his congregation miserable. He was told to stop it.

The experience left a meaningful impression, and when the preacher returned to his body, he never again taught the hell-fire myth.

My favorite story can be found in the book *Destiny of Souls* by Dr. Michael Newton. When the hell-fire preacher arrived in the other dimension, he was greeted by the devil who is described as demonic with a reddish-green face, horns, and wild eyes. In a state of near hysteria, the preacher kept saying, "Why me, why me?" When the experience had its intended effect, his spirit guide removed his devil mask and merely smiled. This intense experience left an indelible imprint on the mind of the preacher.

These experiences provide us with another expanded definition of "we reap what we sow." I believe such an experience would encourage anyone who enjoys scarring people with the burning-hell myth to reconsider the potential consequences of such unnecessary cruelty.

Hell is obviously what we can potentially experience whenever we reincarnate in a physical body.

The means for eliminating the perception associated with repeated body experiences will be explained at the end of this book. It is related to a change in our thinking processes. Heal the mind, and the body will follow.

HUMANS DETERMINE THE OUTCOME

The erroneous belief that God intervenes to help the good guys beat up the bad guys is an ego myth that can have dire consequences. To illustrate these consequences, it is helpful to understand the religious and political turmoil that was taking place in Jerusalem at the time of Yeshua's teachings.

Jewish society, like our contemporary society, contained a variety of conflicting beliefs. The Sadducees rejected the idea of an afterlife; the Pharisees didn't. The Zealots were contentious and believed the Old Testament writings indicated it was time to expel the Romans from the holy city of Jerusalem. Their war message came in conflict with Yeshua's peace message. Yeshua was educated and well-traveled, and he saw firsthand the ferociousness and brutality of the Roman legions. He warned the Zealots that starting a fight with the Romans would result in "not one stone being left upon another in the city."

The Zealots responded by quoting scriptures that they claimed showed how God would bless their righteous cause and help them expel the Roman heathens.

In AD 70 the Zealots led the revolt against the Romans, and by AD 73 "not one stone was left upon another in the city."

It is a myth that God is in the business of intervening in the conflicts of our material world. If He was involved, we wouldn't have experienced the back-to-back world wars of the twentieth century. And to suggest that a perfect, loving God engages in such obvious insanity merely illustrates the convoluted logic of the church of the ego.

How can we be asked to believe that God was involved in any of this insanity when both sides in these world wars professed to be Christian. Hitler attended school for two years at a Benedictine monastery and "dreamed of one day taking Holy Orders." He intended to create a National Church, and the words "Third Reich" translate as the Third Holy Roman Empire. A Christian priest helped edit *Mein Kampf.* These, and many other Christian references, can be found in William L. Shirer's book *The Rise and Fall of the Third Reich.*

To suggest that God was taking sides in this conflict between two opposing groups of Christians merely illustrates how the church of the ego is totally dependent on the concepts of denial, rationalization, minimizing, and projection in its attempt to escape reality.

A) A Native Prophesy

Native American dreamers had a vision that said, "When the Sun goes dark in the seventh month it will be the beginning of the need for a coming together conversation." The marker for this prophesy began in July 1990 with a solar eclipse. The White Bison movement brought indigenous elders from the four corners of the

Earth to Turtle Island (America) for a conference and ceremonies surrounding this prophesy. White Bison study groups continue discussing the teachings associated with this need for harmony.

Although conflict on this planet is thousands of years old, there is a new variable that has been introduced into the experience; nuclear weapons have drastically increased the consequences of conflict.

Several years before this coming-together message, dreamers were having visions of a gourd falling from the sky, and when the gourd split open, dust from it killed everything. They had no idea what this vision meant until news of nuclear explosions and radiation poisoning became public knowledge. Then the answer to the vision became obvious.

This need for a coming-together conversation should be apparent to anyone observing the increased turmoil in the world. Humans are causing it and therefore are responsible for correcting it.

B) Truth or Consequences

The church of the ego teaches that somehow God is involved in directing world affairs. This is an obvious ego projection, and an excuse to avoid accepting the human responsibility for correcting the turmoil. The ego attempts to teach that God is in charge of the material world; therefore it must be His will. But when I observe this ego projection, I know it is unrelated to God's thinking because God does not participate in material conflict.

God is attempting to communicate that this is a human problem unrelated to God's will, and therefore if humans ignore correcting it, it will get worse before it gets better.

C) The Hopi

This is the appropriate place in the narrative to explain the story of the Hopi Nation; the name means peace. I will paraphrase the story in order to avoid writing a four hundred-page book. I apologize to the Hopi elders and ask that they overlook any errors I may make.

Tens of thousands of years ago, civilizations inhabited the Earth. As time passed, conflict between the Peaceful People and the contentious people increased. Abuses became so intense that a cleansing became necessary. A Spirit Guide appeared and led the Peaceful People to a place of safety, and then the Earth was cleansed by fire.

The Peaceful People emerged from their place of safety and civilizations began to spread across the Earth again. Thousands of years passed. But, as before, the people became divided; some were peaceful, and some were contentious. Again the Spirit Guide appeared and placed the Peaceful People in a safe place, and then the Earth was cleansed with ice.

As before, the Peaceful People emerged from their place of safety and spread across the Earth. In time, the contentious people learned to "fly on their shields and destroy one another's cities." The Peaceful People avoided the cities and violence spread. As before, the Spirit Guide appeared and led the Peaceful People to a place of safety. Then the Earth was cleansed by water.

The civilization we now inhabit is the fourth in this series of civilizations. Conditions are becoming as they have been in the past. The Peaceful People and the contentious people are growing further and further apart.

The inhabitants of the Earth may avoid the need for a coming-together conversation, but they cannot avoid the consequences of the mistake.

It is easy for the dominant culture to dismiss the implications of this Hopi story. How could a small group of indigenous elders, living in a semiparched desert, have a better world view than the obviously superior, scientific knowledge of educated Caucasians?

Those who question the validity of the Hopi account concerning three previously advanced societies should pause and ask themselves two questions: First, how is it that every culture on this planet has its version of a flood story? Second, how can Western civilization point to philosophers like Plato as its source for sophistication and, at the same time, ignore the extensive descriptions that Plato gave of a vanished civilization called Atlantis?

The ego has many tricks for preventing us from seeing reality. It's similar to the parable that Yeshua told about the rich man who had great expectations for constructing bigger buildings, expanding his landholdings, and making even larger fortunes. And after mapping out his grandiose plan, he went to sleep that night and didn't wake up the next morning.

D) Harmony or Chaos

Certain traditional Native Americans teach that harmony and balance are achieved when the teachings of the Medicine Wheel are understood and put into practice. I will summarize the particular teachings that I believe apply to the coming-together conversation.

The shortest prayer in the Lakota language is, Mah-toc-ka Oh-yah-see, which translates as " all my relations." ". Its expanded meaning is: I am related to every living thing. In other words, if it is alive then it is part of the Creator. We need to see living things as Wakan (sacred).

The colors that are placed on the four directions of the Wheel are red, yellow, black, and white. This means there is only one race, the human race. It comes in many colors, but they are all relatives from the same Creator.

Science is now verifying this oneness principle. DNA traces everyone on the planet to a common ancestor; we are, in fact, all relatives just as the Medicine Wheel says. This interesting concept of DNA chemistry also tells us that believing we are separate individuals is an illusion. You and I are composites of our parents DNA, our grandparents DNA, our great-grandparents DNA, and so on. The belief that I am a separate, unique person is a fantasy; DNA chemistry verifies this conclusion.

Considering current DNA science, we may want to ask if the Medicine Wheel teachings appear to be ancient knowledge or are they advanced knowledge? This is where it might be helpful to re-call our previous reference to a Native American Wisdom Teacher who lived at the confluence of the Missouri and Mississippi Rivers a thousand years before Europeans invaded Turtle Island.

When Europeans crossed the ocean and began colonizing the Americas, they brought with them a different way of thinking and behavior. Upon observing these behaviors, Native American elders warned the Natural People to avoid learning the new ways. The elders said, "They beat their children, they disrespect their women, and they lie and cheat one another; this is not the path to harmony."

Those who heard this warning said, "Why then did the Creator allow these people to cross the ocean and bring their bad habits here?" The elders smiled and said, "Because the Creator wants us to teach them how to be Natural Human Beings."

E) The Stalemate

As long as the church of the ego is the dominant force on this plan-et, the belief in separation and judgment will prevent any mean-ingful coming-together conversation. The ego pretends to have these conversations, but because it values winning and dominance more than it values justice and fairness, the talks are meaningless.

The church of the ego claims it receives its instructions from a thousand-page history book they call the Bible. In that book, the Teacher of Peace is recorded as saying, "Treat others the way you want to be treated," and "Judge not; for the judgment you make is the judgment you will receive, and the measure you give will be the measure you get." These two teachings are obviously related to the statement, "You reap what you sow." The ego doesn't believe these teachings and has no idea what they mean.

The other interesting revelation found in the Peace Teacher's remarks is that these teachings are directly focused on human behavior as the catalyst for peace. There is no attempt in these teachings to say, as the ego would have us believe, that God has direct responsibility for this peace process. The responsibility rests directly with the beliefs and behaviors of the people of this planet.

I have yet to meet a person who has perfected the art of treating others the way they want to be treated. Socrates perceived this same problem when he asked how we can pretend to talk about Heaven when we haven't yet learned how to be civilized here on Earth?

The original thoughts of the Buddha echo the same logic. How can we pretend to know the mind of a perfect Creator while our own imperfect behavior renders us incapable of such a conversation? This is also why Buddhism is considered a philosophy; it avoids pretentiousness by being nontheistic. Buddhism strives for perfection or enlightenment but perceives that the unenlightened mind does not possess the means or ability to describe or define the mind of the Deity.

This is also why the Bible is a flawed attempt to define the Mind of God; human egos are involved in the process. The Bible is the product of a split mind; one part is ego dominated and the other part is tutored by the Spirit. The ego part is easy to detect when we understand the split-mind concept. Anything describing attack, revenge, separation, or jealousy is from the lower half of the mind. In contrast, the Spirit part teaches love, joy, peace, patience, and forgiveness.

Believing that these diametrically opposed thinking systems are compatible reveals the ego trick of reaction formation—the belief that the mind can contain two opposing viewpoints and still remain internally serene.

The Bible contains practical examples of this split-mind concept. At Exodus 20, the Spirit tells Moses, "Do not build an altar of chiseled stone, and do not approach it by steps." A few decades later, the ego has altered the concept, and we find elaborate temples with altars of chiseled stone that are approached by many steps. This ego error began at Solomon's temple and continued uninterrupted all the way to the church architecture of today.

At Deuteronomy 17:16, the Spirit tells Moses that if the people ask for a king, "The king must not acquire many horses for himself, and he must not acquire many wives for himself, and he must not acquire in great quantity silver and gold for himself. And neither should he exalt himself above other members of the community." (The Spirit instructed Moses to record this law in anticipation of what the Spirit knew would eventually happen.)

The ego obviously ignored this message, and a few generations later, we see the ego reverse the story as the kings of Israel turn the Spirit's instructions upside down with a display of opulence that will set in motion the next two thousand years of Christian history. The kings and queens of Europe were delighted to accept the ego's version of this mistake and proceeded to ravage Europe with their greed. In the thousands of pages of comments concerning European history, I have never read one reference to the Spirit part of this story, but the ego part was told by both kings and priests as if it were the truth.

The Spirit gives a clear warning as to the consequences for ignoring the rules spelled out at Deuteronomy 17. At I Samuel 8:11, the Spirit summarizes the consequences that will transpire if the ego is allowed to replace the Spirit rules: "The king that will reign over you will take your sons for his military, he will have some of them plow his ground and reap his harvest, and make his weapons for war. He will take your daughters to be cooks and bakers. He will take the best of your fields and vineyards, and orchards and give them to his courtiers. He will take your male and female slaves and the best of your cattle. He will tax everything and you will become his slaves."

As I review the history describing the thinking and behavior of the kingdoms and governments on this planet, I see them acting out everything that the Spirit clearly warned would happen if the ego was in charge. This is also how we can discern that claiming to follow the Church of the Spirit does not make it so, and the "divine right of kings" was an obvious invention of the church of the ego. It is also revealing that no Christian historian or theologian ever quoted the true Spirit messages that are recorded at Exodus 20 or Deuteronomy 17, and at the same time, they conveniently ignored the warnings at I Samuel 8.

When the Spirit said, "The altar should not be approached by steps," it was a metaphorical way of saying all humans are spiritually equal and therefore those approaching the altar should not exalt themselves above others. The passage at Deuteronomy 17:20 plainly says that even a king is forbidden to "exalt himself above other members of the community." These are clear Spirit messages of equality that contradict any ego notion of class distinction or hierarchy.

Can you imagine the consequences if a sixteenth-century monk or theologian said such a thing to a king or priest? The threat of being burnt at the stake had a chilling effect on anyone daring to make reference to the truth. The ego enforcement of its teachings through the use of terror and intimidation should be reason enough to realize that it is the opposite of the Spirit.

Fresh water and brine do not come forth from the same source. The ego obviously had a hand in assembling some of the stories in the Bible, and the consequences for humanity continue to be experienced as the Spirit clearly warned.

Another example of a Spirit message that the ego has altered is found at Deuteronomy 14. This passage explains the true meaning of the tithe; it is a lesson in thrift and social security.

Deuteronomy 14:23 clearly says that the tithe of your grain, wine, oil, and the firstlings of your herd or flock that you have saved up all year "you shall eat in the presence of the Lord at the appointed place. And if that appointed place is far from your home you can convert the tithe into money and then carry the money to the appointed place where you can spend the money for whatever you wish; oxen, sheep, wine, strong drink—or whatever you desire."

Every third year you shall bring the tithe to your towns and store it in order to share it with the Levites, alien residents, orphans, and widows."

These passages clearly describe the tithe as a celebration and also as a means of sharing with those in need. The only "church" concept is described with the tithe of the "third year" when it is shared with the Levites. These Levites are appointed to teach and administer the law and therefore do not have land holdings or means to grow their own food.

I will leave it to the readers to decide if their understanding of the word tithe has come from the teachings of the ego or the teachings of the Spirit.

F) Which Bible

Yeshua explains the greatest of the commandments at Matthew 22:37 where he says, "First you should love God with all your heart, soul, and mind; and the second, you should love your neighbor as yourself. Upon these two principles hang all the law and prophets."

These are obviously principles of the Church of the Spirit. And at Galatians 5:22, we are told that the fruits of the Spirit are, "Love, joy, peace, patience, kindness."

As we follow this thread of truth, we find that this theme of love is the key to perceiving the Spirit's presence. This is because we are told that God is love at Galatians 4:16. So it is logical that the Spirit Voice for God would teach only love.

We are also told how to recognize the presence of the ego at Galatians 4:18 where we read, "There is no fear in love, because perfect love casts out fear, for fear has to do with punishment."

There are many other passages that illustrate both the messages of the Spirit and the messages of the ego. The Bible is the product of the split mind. It contains both the love messages and the separation or fear messages. When I perceive the difference, I have no problem understanding the two opposing viewpoints.

The English language can cause confusion concerning the meaning of the word *love*. For instance, in the Greek language, there are three distinctions: eros or erotic love, philos or brotherly love, and agape or principled love. The psychologist, Carl Rogers, provides us with an understandable definition when he describes love as "unconditional, positive regard."

No matter how we attempt to define the word love, there is no way it can be confused with any of the shame, guilt, and separation messages that the church of the ego has contributed to the Bible. And when someone says it is difficult to make sense out of the Bible because it contradicts itself, they are obviously perceiving the presence of the two opposing voices in the writings. We can solve this confusion by removing or ignoring anything that clouds the perception of love's presence.

Thomas Jefferson, the third president of the United States, understood the contradictions of these opposing Bible voices, and he removed all the blocks to love's presence by composing his own Bible. He copied all the references to the love teachings and removed all the references to the teachings of separation, judgment, and fear. This was obviously a radical idea for his particular time in history; consequently, he avoided revealing his private thoughts.

There is one more important point to be made concerning the ego's ability to turn the meaning of scripture upside down. The next chapter will illustrate the ego defense of projection—the desire to escape our personal feelings of guilt by projecting them onto someone or something else. This scapegoat mechanism is as ancient as human history.

THE SCAPEGOAT

Throughout antiquity human sacrifice was used to appease the gods. It was a preferred practice to use captured slaves as the victim. It wasn't difficult to convince the citizens of the community that a foreign slave was a better choice than one of the members of the community. But wasting valuable slave labor eventually became an issue, and some inventive priest decided that animals could be a good substitute. This priest also suggested that the animal's blood was the life force that pleased the gods, and this technical slight-of-hand made it possible for the priest to pour out the blood in order to complete the sacrifice and then divide the carcass between his family and the family of the donor. It seemed like a very civilized way to appease the gods and also benefit the donor as well as the priest. It was a rather easy sell because everyone seemed to benefit except the goat.

There are references in the Old Testament to this pagan practice of human sacrifice. At Deuteronomy 12:30, the Spirit is instructing Moses to warn the Jewish community to avoid the pagan neighbor's practice of "burning their sons and daughters in the fire to their gods." The Spirit emphasized that God considered this practice to be abhorrent. Moses's warning seemed to fade over time, and several decades later, we hear the prophet Jeremiah (7:31) reprimanding certain members of the community for picking up bad habits from the pagans. Unfortunately, the practice of burning their sons and daughters in the fire found its way into parts of the community.

Jeremiah emphatically says, "God never commanded such things and it never entered His mind to even think such things." This account seems to contradict the belief in the burning hell we find in the New Testament because God would never think to burn any of His children in fire, but the ego would.

Projecting guilt onto someone or something external to itself is the ego's most important means of survival. It's a very convoluted concept used by the church of the ego; it convinces people that they are guilty and then claims it knows how to use projection to remove the guilt. The real confusion in this process comes from the wide variety of things we are supposed to be guilty of; the list is never ending, and it differs from culture to culture. The church of the ego adds to this confusion by introducing the concept of "original sin." We are told that when Adam and Eve listened to the serpent, their sin not only killed them but also killed all the rest of us who had nothing to do with the crime. The church of the ego has ensured the need for its existence by teaching these two sources of guilt—that long list of dos and donts and that ancient curse of a crime we didn't commit.

Imagine the panic that would set in if the ego was told that its belief in guilt is a myth and there is no legitimate need for the ego's use of projection to rid itself of guilt.

It's important to explain that the belief in guilt is an error in perception, but this error in perception is not real. (Explaining the logic of this statement requires too many additional pages. The reference material at the end of this book will provide a through explanation.)

Since the church of the ego's existence depends on the perception of guilt, it has manipulated several parts of the Bible in order to substantiate its belief systems.

Referring back to our previous mention of the teaching that the life force is in the blood, the ego expands this perception by saying, "Without the shedding of blood, there is no forgiveness of sin."

The Spirit is familiar with this ego belief, but the Spirit is more intelligent than the ego and uses the ego's statements to uncover the inconsistency and instability of the ego's thought systems.

A perfect example of this ego inconsistency is revealed in the book of Leviticus where we see many scriptures describing grain offerings as sacrifices for sin. These passages make it obvious that grain is also a method of sin sacrifice, and grain clearly contains no blood it can shed.

This contradicting difference between the ego's teachings of blood sacrifice and the reality teachings of the Spirit are illustrated by the following scriptures: Psalm 50:14 (RSV translation), "Make thanksgiving your sacrifice to God." Psalm 40:6, "God, sacrifice and offerings you do not desire...burnt offerings and sin offerings you have not required." Psalm 51:1, "Have mercy on me, O God, according to your steadfast love; according to your abundant mercy blot out my transgressions." Yeshua said, "Go and learn what this means, 'I desire mercy not sacrifice'" (Matt. 9:13). He also said,"But if you had known what this means, 'I desire mercy not sacrifice,'you would not have condemned the guiltless" (Matt. 12:7).

At Psalm 50, the Spirit describes the absurdity of believing that God needs anything material from humans. The whole theme of the Psalms and Prophets is that it is our behavior toward other human beings that is important and to believe that the Sovereign of the Universe is somehow appeased by bribery, or sacrifice should demonstrate the distorted thinking of the ego. It's a human characteristic to solicit bribes, and any ego attempt to project this imperfection onto the Sovereign of the Universe clearly reveals the ego's involvement in the process.

There are several interconnected ego tricks associated with its belief in human sacrifice. It's necessary to examine the individual errors before we attempt to show how they have been promoted as truth.

In AD 326 the theologians at the First Council of Nicaea were instructed by the Roman Emperor Constantine to compose a church doctrine that was compatible with the various religions of the empire. These scholars were well versed in the Greek classics and trained in logic and rhetoric; the results of their scholarship have persisted for centuries.

There were three theological tasks they knew they had to complete. First, they had to prove Jesus was God; second, they had to show he was a sin sacrifice; and third, they had to convince the subjects of the empire that the members of the council were God's authority on Earth.

The first task of proving that Jesus was God was linked to the pagan belief that human sacrifice and the shedding of blood was a means of atonement for sin. This sacrifice had to be perfect and therefore couldn't be a real human, because all humans were infected with original sin. This sounds like scholarly logic, but it has some serious flaws. Starting with a false premise can never lead to a true conclusion.

Attempting to make Jesus into God sparked the first violent debates at the council. Greek and Roman polytheists had no problem with the concept. After all, Julius Caesar was a god, Nero was a god, and Caesar Augustus was a god. There were several Greek/ Roman myths that said, "The god they worshiped had died for them, had risen from the grave; and would, if appealed to by faith and ritual, save them from hell, and share with them his gift of eternal life." (Durant). This is a Greek myth.

The monotheists objected to the idea that humans could kill God. They said the concept was absurd. And the scriptures say that no man has ever seen God.

The polytheists reminded the monotheists that Caesar was a god and he died. This exchange of words was monitored by the Roman Emperor Constantine who was known to be intolerant of anyone or anything that impeded the welfare of the empire. Suggesting that Caesar wasn't a god was not the most prudent position to take in these debates.

These arguments became physically violent. But eventually the majority thought it prudent to vote for the concept of the mystery of the trinity. Jesus was made God, and if there were questions about this obvious contradiction of scripture, they were dismissed as a mystery beyond human comprehension.

The first line of the beginning of John's gospel says, "In the beginning was the word, and the word was with God, and the word was God." This obviously makes it sound like Jesus is God. But this is a manipulation of the translation. This very same chapter clearly says, "No man has seen God." (v. 18). This habit of tampering with Bible translation is revealed at 1 John 5:7 in the King James translation where we read, "There are three that bear record in Heaven; the Father, the word, and the Holy Ghost, and these three are one. This Father, Son, Holy Ghost scripture is supposed to be a proof text for the trinity doctrine." But there is a major flaw in this text: a note by Scofield says, "It is generally agreed that verse 7 has no real authority, and has been inserted."

Since this altered version of trinity is the corner stone of the church of the ego for establishing its authority, it's necessary to thoroughly examine the subject in order to correct this authority error.

Another proof text that suggests Jesus is God is found at John 10:30 where Jesus says, "The Father and I are one," but reading the remainder of the chapter helps explain why Yeshua had no intention of being God. We can appreciate the importance of true Oneness when Jesus says, "Holy Father, protect them in your name that You have given me, so that they may be One, as we are One." (John 17:11). This is again emphasized at verse 21 where we read, "That they all be One. As You Father are in me and I am in You, may they also be in Us." This Oneness is describing a type of metaphysical DNA; we all, including Yeshua, contain the spiritual DNA of the Father. This is why Jesus said, "Call no one your father on Earth, for you have one Father—the One in Heaven." (Matt. 23:9). The text clearly tells us that we are all children of the Father and therefore spiritually equal. This solves the authority problem that the ego introduced with the king's and queen's mistake at I Samuel 8:11.

It is also helpful to recall the Spirit warning at Deuteronomy 17:14 that clearly says, "The king should not exalt himself above other members of the community."

One last point about this misinterpretation of the trinity concept: can God have a God? Now this is not a difficult question for a Greek or Roman polytheist; they would say, "Yes, everyone knows that there were lesser gods and greater gods." But a monotheist would vehemently object to such an error by responding, "Hear O Israel, The Lord thy God, The Lord is One." This monotheistic statement is reported to be the hallmark of Jewish contributions to Christine doctrine.

This is where the ego trick of reaction formation becomes obvious. In order to uncover the error we need to understand the chronology of the scriptures.

Between AD 50 and 60, Paul was addressing several of his letters to the Christian congregations by saying, "The God and Father of Jesus." (2 Cor. 1:3; Eph. 1:3; Col. 1:3). So Paul clearly knew Jesus had a God, and God was the Father and Jesus was the Son.

The chronology here is important because Paul, the monotheist, knew nothing of the theological changes that would be made 250 years later at the Council of Nicaea. He understood that God was the Father and Jesus was the Son, and to believe that the son could be his own father is ridiculous.

Jesus himself says he has a God at Revelation 3:12, and he repeats that four times. The only "mystery" in this confusion is revealed by the ego's attempt to fabricate one.

The ego needs this authority confusion because its church is founded on doctrines totally opposite the Oneness Principle. This is the reason the ego defense of reaction formation is necessary. This defense suggests we can be spiritually equal and at the same time be spiritually unequal. This is also where the separation theology of Greek/Roman mythology concerning the devil and the demons enters the story.

The ego does not intend to give up without a fight, and it finds it quite convenient to use concepts from Greek/Roman myth in order to support the split-mind concept of the reaction formation. The devil and the demons now become the scapegoats for the theological confusion of separation and attack. This clearly violates the Oneness Principle. The devil is a mythological invention designed to obscure ego-orientated thinking. The statement "The devil made me do it" is a good example of attempts to project our guilt onto something external to ourselves. When we eventually perceive our guiltlessness, it is no longer necessary to ask the ego for help. This is the real meaning of "The truth will set you free."

It's helpful to remember that the Old Testament contains no mention of a burning hell or a devil with a pitchfork throwing the bad people into the fire. But when the Greek/Roman scholars took over the process of writing the New Testament, we suddenly are entertained with a wide selection of these myths.

We all have to choose which Wolf we feed, and we are totally in charge of that choice. The lower part of the split mind is susceptible to the voice of the ego. The higher part of the mind is the domain of the Spirit. The ego's voice is loud and demanding. The Spirit voice is soft and confident. The ego knows it has to be loud and demanding in order to keep our attention, because if we learn to listen to the Spirit, the ego will lose its grip and will no longer be able to block our access to serenity and peace.

The next chapter is going to turn the ego perception upside down. And this change in perception will liberate your mind from all the fear messages that the church of the ego has taught you since you took your first earthly breath.

YOU CAN'T EXPLAIN THIS

Socrates said, "Life is a deception, only the soul lives."

Black Elk said, "This world is only a shadow of the real World."

Einstein said, "Man's experience is an optical delusion of his consciousness."

Stephen Hawking said, "What we call real time is just a figment of our imagination; it exist only in our minds."

The *Book of Genesis* says, "God caused a deep sleep to fall upon Adam"—but nowhere does the Bible refer to Adam waking up.

Up to this point in my rambling narrative, I can imagine the ego saying, "Yes but..." The above quotes make it difficult for anything the ego teaches to be able to invent its next "yes but." The ego can't explain these quotes because if the ego understood how to explain them, it would disappear. This is why the Spirit is confident that It will heal the split mind, because the Spirit knows how to explain these quotes, and the ego doesn't have a clue.

A) Neither View Will Do

There are two opposing schools of thought that contend for our allegiance and belief in modern society. Religious creationists claim they have a sacred book that explains how God created the Heavens and the Earth. In contrast, scientific evolutionist claim that the fossil record demonstrates tangible proof of natural selection and the appearance of *Homo sapiens*. Neither of these beliefs can adequately explain the origin of the mind.

When religionists say they believe God is perfect and eternal, they automatically contradict their claim that God created the Heavens and the Earth because a perfect, eternal God is incapable of creating temporal imperfection; it's a contradiction in definitions. Everything material, including the universe, is in a state of decay and therefore not the product of a perfect, eternal Creator. It's an ego trick that will be explained later.

What then are we to say about evolution? I asked a scientist to explain this question: "When the ameba turned into an amphibian, and the amphibian turned into a vertebrate, and the vertebrate turned into *Homo sapiens*, why didn't one of these organisms think to eliminate the death gene?" The scientist smiled and said, "There is no thinking in this process; that's what natural selection is all about." I then said, "Excellent, if the ameba didn't think, and the amphibian didn't think, at what point in this selection process did thinking appear, and what caused it?" I could tell by the look on his face that he had never previously considered such a question.

Scientists are desperately trying to link the evolution of the brain to the concept of mind, but they can't make the two fit because the mind and the brain are not the same. The brain is a part of the body and therefor can't be the mind.

A diligent search of the teachings of the philosophers of the last three thousand years will demonstrate how the most brilliant and logical thinkers of history have yet to arrive at a consensus as to the origin and composition of the mind.

A common example of the mind mystery can be observed with the placebo effect. When scientists select a test and control group to verify the effectiveness of a new drug treatment, they give one group the drug and the other group sugar pills. The placebo effect is observed when some of the people in the sugar pill group have a positive outcome; their mind responded to the suggestion.

There is a process called meta-analysis where the statistical results of a large number of experiments are mathematically averaged. This averaging shows that the placebo effect is as effective as drug treatment. Pharmaceutical companies are obviously not interested in funding research concerning the enhancement of placebo treatment.

In the book *Healing Words*, by Dr. Larry Dossey, there is an account of a series of drug experiments where the belief of the scientist affected the outcome of the experiment. In other word, if the scientist believed that the test patients would have a positive outcome, they did. And if the scientist didn't believe the drug would be effective, it wasn't. Dr. Dossey wrote this book in 1993, and it contained a wide variety of examples of how the mind is involved in the healing processes.

Since there is little commercial profit to be made by teaching people how to use their mind to heal their bodies, there is little interest in pursuing this process.

Another interesting book illustrating the mind processes is *The Conscious Universe* by Dr. Dean Radin. His experiments are interesting because he employs the process of meta-analysis to demonstrate the statistical significance associated with a wide variety of mind studies.

Dr. Radin gave an amusing description of the ridged orthodoxy within the scientific community that inhibits the acceptance of new discoveries. He observed that when a new anomaly is reported by a research study, the orthodox community shows little interest in this contradiction to the status quo. But the scientists, who see potential significance in the anomaly, continue to pursue an explanation; this process can continue for decades. Dr. Radin commented that eventually the anomaly is explained and becomes an accepted part of scientific understanding, and then the original skeptics claim they discovered the process.

The ego presents itself in many unexpected places.

In our next chapter, we are going to introduce another illustration of logic that reveals why belief in the ego is truly an illusion.

The ego believes it is powerful and consequently those who listen to it are deluded into believing they are also powerful. If you are a member of the church of the ego, you are about to have your world turned upside down.

It has been reasonably easy for ego logic to contradict much of what has been written up to this point in the narrative. You are now about to experience why there are no more "yes buts" in the ego's bag of tricks.

Fasten your seatbelt, you are about to experience zero gravity.

MOUSE EYES, EAGLE EYES

There is a Native American story called the Jumping Mouse. It is a long story, and therefore I am going to shorten the story by summarizing the details.

Unless a person understands the overall dynamics of the Star Trail story of chapter 6, it would be difficult to discern how the metaphors in the Jumping Mouse are directly related to the Star Tail ending. Nevertheless, they are the same story told in two different ways.

The conclusion of the Jumping Mouse adventure takes place when the mouse willingly gives up his mouse eyes and turns into an eagle.

Eagle eyes can see much further ahead than those who choose to stay confined to mouse eyes.

A) It's Not Really That Big

It would be helpful for the reader to obtain a few props in preparation for beginning our mind trip into eternity. You already have the props; they are ordinary household items, but it's best

74

you have them in front of you before we begin. All you need is a nickel and a large dinner plate. I will wait here while you go get them.

The ego is telling you not to do it because it is scared out of its wits that what you are about to experience will change your mind about the power of the ego.

I am going to make a cup of tea now while you get the nickel and the plate.

The mathematical scale of this illustration is not important, but the concept is very important. Your mind is about to experience eternity, and you are now going to understand what Socrates, Black Elk, Einstein, and Hawking were describing when they said, "This world is an illusion."

To begin, I want you to look at the period at the end of this sentence. Now imagine that period represents our entire solar system—the sun, and all the planets.

Now pick up that nickel you have in front of you, and look at it carefully. It represents our Milky Way galaxy, our sun and planets are out toward the edge of that nickel, and the Milky Way we observe in the sky at night is the edge of our galaxy.

Now pick up that dinner plate, and picture it containing millions of galaxies. You are now holding the entire universe in your hand.

A scientist named Hubble discovered that the universe is expanding; this is called the red-shift. If you need details look it up on the net.

It's necessary to introduce the concept of the red-shift because this is where our illustration is going to differ from current scientific speculation. But for illustration purposes, let's say that the dinner plate you are holding expands to twice its size or maybe even three times its size, it makes no difference because everything beyond that plate you are holding is eternity—all the space in the room, all the space beyond the room; all the space in the city, state, and country. That dinner plate represents the mouse eye view. All the space in the room and outside the room represents the Eagle Eye view. There is a very big difference between the small, material universe and the never-ending vastness of eternity.

Eternity is where God is; and since God is love, the whole universe (that dinner plate) is totally surrounded by love. Love is the only reality. The universe (that dinner plate) is like a cocoon surrounded by love. Everyone inside the cocoon is asleep and going through a slow transition. When the butterfly wakes up, the cocoon will no longer have a purpose.

Now try to convince me that God needs me to give Him some material object for atonement or to please Him. God has no perception of what that even means. That whole dinner plate of those millions of galaxies doesn't even exist if I am standing a hundred miles away in eternity. A perfect, loving God is waiting in eternity for His sons and daughters to wake up and return to where they belong.

We will tell a story later to explain how we are tricked by the ego into coming back to our incarnation experiences in the Earth School.

Remember the Star Trail story where the goal is to enter Paradise. The goal is not to keep coming back to the Earth School. This is why it is important to learn what Yeshua taught, because the purpose of his wisdom is mind training. This is why he taught that we are to "have the mind of Christ." This is the difference between the Church of the Spirit and the church of the ego. One is of the higher mind, and one is of the lower mind. Higher gets you where you want to be; lower gets you nothing but pain, disappointment, and death. The ego is a bad choice.

B) Limits

The big bang is our best illustration of limits. Some very brilliant, scientific work has revealed the beginning of our material universe. (That dinner plate you are holding.) Here again, it would be cumbersome to explain the details of the process. Nevertheless, experts in mathematics, astrophysics, quantum and particle physics, and so on combine their knowledge to be able to run our current movie back to where it all started fourteen billion years ago. Actually, the theory of general relativity breaks down a few nanoseconds before we reach the exact beginning. (Later in this chapter, we will use Zeno's Paradox to explain why this happens.)

This big bang process is important for illustrating limits because there is nothing previous to that fourteen billion-year-ago beginning. Science is at a dead end. Science cannot test anything beyond that zero point, because science has nothing physical before that zero to weigh, measure, or touch.

Currently there are many theories trying to guess at alternatives. There is quite a list: string theory, multiuniverses, parallel universes, dark matter, super symmetry, and so on. The problem for any of these theories is obvious; we have reached the limit of our ability to test them. For example, the particle accelerator at Geneva Switzerland is at a practical limit for what humans can construct and operate. The length of the acceleration tunnel combined with the amount of power necessary to bring it to working speed has reached a limit. People in the science business already know this.

C) Zeno's Paradox

A few thousand years ago a Greek philosopher named Zeno amuse himself by asking questions that tended to aggravate those of his colleagues who didn't have a sense of humor. For instance, how long will it take you to walk from one side of a room to the opposite side? But before we start, there are certain rules we need to follow. Step one: we walk half the distance to the wall and stop.

Step two: we proceed from this point to walk half the distance to the wall and stop. Step three: now we proceed from this point to walk another half. It doesn't take long before we realize that we are never going to make it to the other wall. We may get very close, but never quite get there. This is why General Relativity breaks down a few nanoseconds before we reach the big bang zero point.

Science has encountered these kinds of limits many times. Several decades ago there were attempts in the laboratory to reach absolute zero (−273 degrees Celsius). Experimenters got extremely close, but were never able to reach the actual zero point.

This is also why the length of a particle accelerator, in relation to the amount of power to operate it, has reached a practical limit. And this practical limit also defines a limit to the exploration of particle physics.

This problem is also encountered in theoretical physics when mathematical calculations result in the solution being expressed as infinity.

A more practical illustration of limits is expressed when the human body is found to be incapable of long-distance space travel. For millions of years, our bodies have learned to function under the influence of Earth's gravity. This has established a natural limit for the human body. This is the real reason the US space program lost momentum. Scientists were the first to realize that *Star Wars* was a Hollywood fantasy and unrelated to reality.

This is also how we know that the universe has several things that define its limits. The most well-understood limit is the speed of light at 186,000 feet per second. There are desperate attempts to overcome this limit, but as of this writing, the attempts have failed.

Einstein's suggestion that space-time has a curvature also defines a limit. That is why that dinner plate that we used to illustrate the universe has a round edge. The curvature of space-time is the circular edge of the plate. The universe isn't linear; it's curved.

The material universe is also going to disappear; all the stars will eventually burn out, including our sun. That is when we will all be back in eternity where we really belong.

D) The Chemistry Set

The story I am about to tell is a modern adaptation of the parable of the Prodigal Son found in the New Testament book of Luke. It is a metaphorical attempt to ease the mind of the reader into perceiving the origin of the material universe and time. We will reveal the source of the exact details later, but turning the ego mind upside down needs to be done slowly in order to minimize the shock.

Once upon a time there was a prominent chemist; he was an expert. The chemist wanted his son to follow in his footsteps, so he gave the son an elaborate chemistry set. The son was thrilled. The father reminded the son that it would be best for the son to do his experiments outside in order to prevent any mistakes from damaging the home. The son understood the wisdom of the rules and totally agreed.

In the course of time, the son was making a thorough search of all the information contained in the book that came with the chemistry set. One day he came across a chapter titled "explosives." He was a teenage boy and was anxious to experiment with this information. Then he recalled his agreement with the father to do the experiments outside, just in case of mistakes. But the son realized that if the father saw him mixing up explosives, it may not be something the father would approve. The son solved the problem by taking his experiment down to a secluded spot in the basement. The plan seemed to be working well until the son blew up part of the basement. He was mortified. What will my father say when he sees I disobeyed the rules? Overcome with guilt, the son packed his bags, bought a bus ticket, and left home.

When the father came home from work and saw the damage, he was alarmed. He searched through the rubble looking for his son and was relieved to find no sign of his son being injured. Then he realized the son was probably embarrassed for breaking the rules, and he ran away. The father employed a detective to find the son and to tell the son that everything is OK and that the son needed to return home.

As time went by, the teenage son was finding it difficult to survive in the world. He worked long hours for minimum wages, he lived in a dangerous neighborhood, and he never seemed to have enough to eat. Eventually, his desperation overcame his fear and guilt, and he decided to go home and face the consequences.

As the son was walking down the street toward his home, the father had come outside to collect the morning newspaper. When he saw the son approaching, he rushed down the sidewalk, hugged the son, and said everything is OK.

The father and the son went inside and celebrated the homecoming.

That explosion that the son made while experimenting with his chemistry set is comparable to the origin of the big bang. If the similarity sounds confusing, the reader will eventually be given sufficient information to totally comprehend the analogy.

E) The Multiplex Theater

One last story is necessary in order to explain the use of the word illusion in relation to the material universe. It's helpful to remember that I am only illustrating what Socrates, Black Elk, Einstein, and Hawking said: the material world is an illusion.

The Star Trail story in chapter 6 can be misunderstood as describing reincarnation; however, the multiplex theater story will explain how the transmigration of the soul is actually an illusion that merely appears to be real.

Most of us have attended a multiplex movie theater at some time in our lives. There is a long hallway with signs above the entrances directing us to a selection of movies. We walk down the hallway until we find the specific movie we paid to see. Then we take our popcorn and chocolate-covered raisins into the theater and find a comfortable seat. The lights go dim, the music starts, and the romance begins. A young couple are hugging, kissing, and strolling along the seashore at sunset. As the story progresses, the hero gets a good job where he's making lots of money, and the heroine is decorating their new home in preparation for the arrival of their first baby. It's a feel-good movie, and the popcorn and chocolate-covered raisins are great. As time passes we watch the happy family on a yacht sailing into the sunset.

The movie ends, which means we die. But we just take our popcorn and chocolate-covered raisins next door to another movie.

Oh good, this movie looks like another feel-good romance. There is a lovely couple siting in a restaurant, holding hands and staring into each other's eyes. The camera zooms in so we can hear the couple's conversation. It seems that the spouse of one of these lovers is refusing to agree to a divorce and is threating to destroy the person's career if the person leaves. In the course of the conversation, it's revealed that there is a million-dollar life-insurance policy on this uncooperative spouse and the plot thickens. (I have a weak stomach, so I'll skip the part about the hatchet and chain saw.)

A few months later, the happy couple have the million dollars and are thrilled to be together. But down at the police station is a detective who looks something like Columbo. He is pretty smart and begins to piece together the details of the homicide. The next scene is a trick we have seen many times. The two suspects are brought to the police headquarter, placed in separate interrogation rooms, and each one is told that whoever turns state's evidence will escape the death penalty and the other person dies. This partnership is beginning to develop cracks, and we can guess how this movie is not going to end well. This is where we die. But it's no big deal; we just take our popcorn and chocolate-covered raisins next door to another movie.

This time we skip the romantic titles and switch to something that sounds exciting. The movie starts with a tickertape parade in New York City. Bands are playing, people are cheering, and there is a blizzard of confetti drifting down onto a large column of soldiers marching down the street. The wives and children are waving. The soldiers are smiling and happy to be home. Everyone is hugging and kissing, and the excitement of homecoming is heartwarming.

That night a soldier is in bed asleep beside his wife. He begins to have flashbacks in his dreams: people are blown up, some of his buddies are shot, but the part that gets to him is when he rolls that grenade into a room and blows up a bunch of little kids. He wakes up screaming. His wife calms him down. He's going to the VA for PTSD treatment, but his story is beginning to fray around the edges.

These movies are a metaphorical way of depicting projected illusions that we believe are a materially solid world. It's similar to having a dream that feels real or the experience of virtual reality.

We may have been going in and out of these movies for the last thousand years. What we are not consciously aware of are the bits and pieces of truth and reality that the Spirit has been inserting into the scripts. There comes a point where enough of the Spirit perception becomes capable of overcoming the ego perception, and we decide to look for a way out of the theater. That's when we notice there is a sign above a door at the end of the hallway marked "Exit," and we go down the hall and walk out that door into the light of reality.

F) A Scientific Experiment

This may be the most appropriate place in our narrative to disclose the reality of the Spirit and the insanity of the ego.

The ego is tricky and quite talented and has survived for thousands of years by offering convincing excuses for ignoring reality. But the ego is no match for the Spirit, and there is a scientific experiment we can do to reveal this truth.

First we need to review the difference between the Spirit and the ego. The Spirit teaches love, joy, peace, patience, and forgiveness. The ego teaches attack, revenge, resentment, spite, and separation.

All scientific experiments begin with a hypothesis. Then the hypothesis is tested to see if there is evidence that it is true. Our hypothesis contends that the Spirit can remove resentments from our minds, but the ego can't, or won't, because the ego relies on resentments for its existence.

The removal of these resentments is important for our health because resentments held in the mind are poison for the body.

In order to begin the test, we need to choose someone we resent. Perhaps he or she has abused us or did something harmful that has been stuck in our minds for years. This is poisoning us and we need to be rid of it.

Now say, "Holy Spirit, I forgive (Name) and ask that they be given every good thing I would have for myself: health, happiness, prosperity, and love, and please remove the resentment from my mind."

You are not required to have perfect sincerity when you begin this process, but you are required to ask for the Spirit's assistance. How else will our hypothesis be confirmed? Repeat this request every day until you experience the removal of the resentment.

There is only one reason that the resentment isn't removed; it's because you refuse to ask the Spirit to remove it. This is also how we gage how much of a grip the Bad Wolf has on our spirit. The ego is using every excuse in its bag of tricks to convince you that your resentment is unique and shouldn't be forgiven. The ego knows that if you make conscious contact with the Spirit, you will be free. This frightens the ego.

The Church of the Spirit knows the importance of learning true forgiveness because we reap what we sow. Therefore, when we offer forgiveness, we receive forgiveness, and when we offer blessings, we receive blessings.

You have repeated this truth every time you have said, "Our Father, forgive us our trespasses as we forgive those who trespass against us." You have been saying these words for years, but you were never taught how to effectively apply the principle to specific resentments. The ego taught you to say, "I forgive them, but I am not going to forget what they did. They deserve to have something bad happen to them for hurting me."

.This is an ego trick that accomplishes nothing because the resentment stays stuck in my mind, and the poison of the resentment continues to attack the body. The ego believes this type of false forgiveness allows me to drink the poison and expect it to kill the person I resent. This kind of thinking reveals the true insanity of the ego.

This process of true forgiveness is the beginning of the end for the Bad Wolf's control of my spirit. It is also why the church of the ego is incapable of explaining Yeshua's reminder to: "Judge not, because the judgment you render is the judgment you will receive." This truth cannot be explained by the ego, because the ego lives by judgment. And it is also why the ego needs the belief in separation; how else can it find someone to judge? But this ego dependence on separation violates the Oneness Principle explained by Yeshua when he said, "Father, may they be One even as you and I are One." There is a certain irony revealed when someone says, "This oneness is true, but it only applies to Christians." This mistake is obviously ego-inspired, because the fact that it attempts to separate Christians from "others" is pure ego. This ego trick of separation has kept the world in turmoil for the last ten thousand years.

The use of excuses for avoiding the true forgiveness process uncovers the extent to which the ego defenses have controlled my mind. The ego will offer me a variety of "yes buts" that it hopes will prevent me from accessing this simple, but effective, process of true forgiveness.

Dear reader, this is how we learn to give all the correct answers at the end of the Star Trail in order to enter Paradise. These forgiveness lessons are the purpose of our Earth School experiences.

In the next chapter, we are going to explore some things we might consider doing in order to act responsibly while we are still stuck in the illusion.

When Yeshua said, "Your faith can move mountains," he was trying to tell us that the ego is no match for the Spirit. When the mind is Spirit directed, it is able to overcome what appears to be insurmountable obstacles.

NEVER FIRED A SHOT

I s it possible to win a war without firing a shot? The ego says, "No." In contrast, the Spirit says, "There are no true winners in conflict."

We began this book with the axiom: "Thinking leads to behavior; behavior leads to outcome." If we think conflict is inevitable, then it leads us to accept the outcome of conflict as being normal.

We ended the last chapter with the thought that a Spirit-directed mind is capable of moving mountains. The ego believes this is romanticized nonsense. The ego believes that might makes right. The ego says bodies are powerful, and anyone who teaches otherwise is a fool. Whereas, the Spirit says that a mind directed toward true peace can indeed move mountains.

If I said that I could prove that the mind is capable of overcoming empires, what kind of an example would you consider appropriate to offer?

There was a writer and poet named Henry David Thoreau. Many of us remember him from the philosophies he wrote while living in a cabin at the edge of Walden Pond. But how many people are aware that he traveled extensively up and down the East Coast observing the lives and struggles of all sorts of individuals, both rich and poor?

His study of history led him to conclude that the tyranny of a few can control the destiny of the majority, but only if the majority cooperates with the tyrants. He recorded these thoughts in an essay describing the concept of civil disobedience.

His body died of pneumonia at the age of forty-five, but his mind lived on in the thoughts he committed to paper. The mind is more powerful than the body when it is Spirit-directed.

While Thoreau's life was ending in New England, Old England's empire was busy extending the church of the ego into any country vulnerable to its tyranny. India, and its millions of citizens, was feeling the pain of this foreign intrusion.

The greed of ego-driven tyrants impoverishes their victims, and then the ego justifies the tyranny by suggesting that the tyrant's superior intellect and leadership are necessary in order to help the victims recover. It is this kind of convoluted thinking that best illustrates the insanity of the ego.

A handful of tyrants can control millions of victims only if the victims cooperate.

The mind of Thoreau entered the mind of Gandhi. He was an attorney and well read. He knew the wisdom of the *Bhavagad Gita*, Yeshua, and the Buddha. He was a student of the Higher Mind. He understood Thoreau's essay on civil disobedience and decided it was time to stop cooperating with the English tyrants who were wrongfully controlling his country.

In the beginning the tyrants felt confident that their control tactics were capable of insuring their continued success. They were expecting a physical revolt and had the utmost confidence in their military ability to squash such attempts.

Gandhi had no intention of using a physical approach to expelling the English; he knew the mind was more powerful than physical force. He also understood the weakness of an ego whose delusions make it believe it is strong.

In chapter 2, we followed a sequence of events that evolved out of the increased production of the industrial revolution—the need to export excess goods to foreign markets. Gandhi understood this process and instructed his followers to stop buying English cloth. He even encouraged them to weave their own clothing as an alternative. He put away the suits and ties that he previously wore when he practiced law and switched to the dress of the common people in order to illustrate the sincerity of his words.

As stage one of the plan to stop cooperating with the tyrants took effect, the English became alarmed at the depressing result that the boycott had on their revenue.

As the plan of noncooperation began to gain momentum, the success of the plan encouraged millions of Indians to follow the suggestions of Gandhi. The English then became aggressive and, as any ego-directed mind would think to do, they attacked. The police resorted to brutality; Gandhi was jailed several times, but these ego tactics were no match for a Spirit-directed mind.

In a state of frustration at the failure of their brutality, the English decided to change tactics. The ego is always eager to make compromises when its attack plans are ineffective. The English overlords decided to invite Gandhi and his associates to a meeting in order to discuss possible ways to implement mutual cooperation. Gandhi calmly told the English Viceroy and his generals that the English would eventually leave India because the Indian people would never again cooperate with any foreign control of their country. The English were stunned. The ego had convinced them that they were powerful. They believed they possessed the superior talent and ability to build and maintain an orderly empire. How could this bunch of Indian ingrates fail to appreciate the guidance of their English masters?

The inability of the ego to comprehend the logic of its failure is linked to its reliance on denial. Logic and denial are complete opposites.

Gandhi's mind overcame the ego, and the English reluctantly relinquished their control of India.

Gandhi's success frightened every tyrant of the twentieth century by exposing the powerlessness of a minority to control the majority. Gandhi's mind followed the Spirit. It needed no physical army; it employed no guns or aggression, but it did know that a Spirit-directed mind can, in fact, move mountains, something that the church of the ego doesn't understand or even believe.

Gandhi, through his belief in Spirit-led nonviolence, went on to inspire others to follow his example, and they too learned that the ego is no match for the Spirit of Truth and Justice. (*Gandhi* the DVD. is excellent.)

Those who rely on mouse eyes fail to see that the Spirit is slowly replacing the ego. The church of the ego made slavery acceptable for over three thousand years; the Church of the Spirit overturned that belief. The church of the ego burnt witches at the stake for centuries; the Church of the Spirit removed that insanity. For over three thousand years, the church of the ego taught that the divine right of kings was a law from Heaven. The Church of the Spirit removed that error by teaching that Heaven's laws promote equality, acceptance, and justice.

The Spirit has all the time in eternity to accomplish its Peaceful Purpose. Those who see through Eagle Eyes know this is the only reality because reality is changeless, and the Spirit Voice for God is changeless.

The ego's days are numbered, but denial prevents the ego's mouse eyes from seeing this reality.

In our next chapter, we will begin to describe how the path to peace is possible and also how to overcome the ego obstacles that are obviously going to oppose any such attempts to limit its power and control.

THE WILD WEST

S everal decades ago the only law west of the Mississippi River was the law of the jungle. Sam Colt made a living selling the pistol he promoted as the equalizer; in the hands of the little guy, his pistol evened the odds against the big guy.

East of the Mississippi things were more orderly. Gunfights in the streets were not tolerated; local law enforcement was in place to intervene. Law and order was an integral part of the local, state, and federal governance.

As time passed, various Western States began petitioning the federal government for statehood. In order to qualify for consideration, the petitioning state had to have certain basic institutions in place, law and order being one of prime importance.

The Wild West and the law of the jungle faded into history as the United States extended itself all the way to the West Coast. Gunfights in the streets became relics of the past.

If we consider the example of how the Wild West was settled, it becomes obvious that the introduction of effective courts of law at local, state, and federal levels made it possible to prosecute individuals who chose violence as a means of settling disagreements; the benefits of having these institutions in place in order to maintain law and order are observable.

Considering the benefits offered by these arrangements, why isn't there an effective world court in place to prosecute individuals who choose violence as a means for settling disagreements? The key word here is effective.

A) The Elements of Ineffectiveness

The divine right of kings is still in place at the church of the ego; it's disguised by the words "national sovereignty."

If we consider the fact that 1% of the power brokers on this planet control the other 99% of the population, there is no incentive for the people in power to subject themselves to the intervention of an effective world court. This unwillingness to establish an effective court by claiming it interferes with national sovereignty is similar to the excuse used by those who claimed that the US Constitution violated states' rights. In 1862 we fought a Civil War over this issue because some states had an economic interest in resisting the constitutional guarantee of equal rights for all citizens. An analysis of history reveals that the words "economic interest" seem to be a continuing theme for blocking the path to justice and equality; the incentive for maintaining economic interests at the expense of justice and equal rights hasn't changed.

Another ego belief contributing to the chaos on this planet is the result of the power brokers believing they are above the law. This is not only a belief but also an observable condition within the church of the ego.

If the divine right of kings is allowing the 1% to enjoy the benefits of operating above the law, why would the ego want to submit itself to the jurisdiction of an effective world court?

A minor example of this lawlessness is the concept of diplomatic immunity. Who decided that a diplomat can't be prosecuted for committing murder?

Through the process of observation, we have reduced the diagnosis of the problem to its lowest common denominator—the addiction to power and profits. This is the very same addiction that Gandhi observed as the motivation for English imperialism. As in any diagnostic process, we have to identify the disease before we can proceed with a cure.

The time has arrived for applying the Gandhi Principle in order to deprive the addicts of their drug of choice, that is, money, power, and profits.

B) First Things First

There are several pieces to this puzzle, and in order to avoid confusion, we need to examine each of the pieces to understand how they are linked together.

The church of the ego tries to convince us that we are weak. But logic says that 99% is not weaker than 1%. When Gandhi got the mind of the 99% going in the same direction, the 1% disappeared.

In chapter 4, we looked at the consequences of overpopulation; it is not ecologically sustainable, and it is also the prime motivation for war. These consequences require our willingness to help change the trend.

People can do their individual part by practicing reasonable family planning. With modern contraception, this should be rather easy. But the church of the ego joins with businessmen, religion, and politicians to block our access to contraception. When we identify individuals or institutions that interfere with our right to choose, we need to withdraw our support from anyone or anything that disrespects that right. If you support them, you are giving them the power to take away your rights. They claim they know what's best, but if overpopulation is killing the planet, how can it be the best?

The 1% decided to defund Planned Parenthood, but if the 99% sent Planned Parenthood a few dollars, it would demonstrate how weak the 1% is. This is simple logic. There are over 300 million people in America. If only 150 million sent Planned Parenthood a dollar, the few million dollars that the church of the ego withdrew would be insignificant.

The same logic applies to the American Civil Liberties Union. The church of the ego hates the ACLU for the same reason the ego hates your free access to truth. Truth uncovers the tyranny and trickery of the ego. The ego cannot function in the clear light of day. That is why the ACLU's dedication to protecting the Constitution and your civil rights is our most important protection against the tyranny of the 1%. This is why the ego is constantly attacking the ACLU by trying to convince the public that the ACLU is unnecessary.

A practical example as to why protecting the Bill of Rights and free speech is of utmost importance can be understood by the fact that four hundred years ago, the contents of this book would result in my being burnt at the stake and not just me dear reader but also you for reading or even possessing the book.

The church of the ego hates the Constitution and the Bill of Rights; the ego has no perception of equality or justice, and when truth uncovers the trickery of the ego, it resorts to terror.

C) Remember the Gandhi Principal

The Gandhi Principle is not complicated. All that is necessary is to identify the things that feed the ego of imperialism and then stop participating in them. But first we need to identify the illness.

What is meant by the term "consumerism"? Since it's called an *ism*, it must be a certain kind of belief. This belief concept brings us back to the axiom that thinking leads to behavior, and behavior leads to outcome.

We need to examine how the ego trains our thinking to believe in consumerism, and we need to ask if this belief leads to a positive outcome.

Let's begin with something we are all familiar with, commercials on TV. How are these commercials designed to influence our thinking? They try to convince us that in order to be happy, healthy, and wise, we need to buy their product. Such a suggestion sounds good, but it reminds me of the conversation Eve had with that snake. Eve said the snake convinced her that what it was selling was "good for food, pleasing to the eyes, and designed to make one wise." We all know the outcome. The snake's salesmanship killed Eve. This is similar to the commercial that tempts me with an oversize hamburger and large fries, everything I need to cause an epidemic of type 2 diabetes. Or, how about that good-looking girl sitting on the hood of that $60,000 truck that helps the banker gobble up every penny of my paycheck. But my eventual bankruptcy was worth it because my ego was flying high for a few months.

The message of every commercial, whether it's selling toothpaste or a trip to Acapulco, is that you won't be happy until you have what the commercial is selling. These companies and their commercials aren't interested in your happiness. They are after your hard-earned money. Ben Franklin said it best when he observed that a fool and his money are soon parted. There are no victims in this process, just volunteers.

If you listen to the snake, the consequences are on you, not the snake. Don't feed the snake, and he will die.

D) Minimize and Downsize

In chapter 7, we recorded the scriptures where the Spirit told Moses that any king of Israel was not to accumulate a lot of horses, wives, gold and silver, and so on, and he was not to exalt himself above other members of the community. A similar message was repeated by Yeshua in the New Testament when he reminded us that the pursuit of extravagant wealth does not produce a peaceful heart.

Somewhere along the path of time, the ego turned this Spirit message upside down. The church of the ego teaches that those who possess wealth and opulence are blessed by God; their wealth is visible proof of God's favor. With this kind of thinking, it is also possible to conclude that if you are poor then God must hate you. And if God hates you, then it's OK if I hate you too. This path of ego thinking is a slippery slope to serious error.

Money is neither good nor bad, but being addicted to excessive amounts of it is the sign of an ego-inspired sickness. This obsession is revealed when the addict is unable to offer a logical answer to the question, "How much is enough?"

In 1968 I lived in a comfortable two-bedroom house that only required a sixty amp electric service. In the twenty-first century, we are taught we need a four-bedroom house with three bathrooms and a three hundred amp electric service. We are not only taught that we need this excessive space but we also believe we will die if we can't have it.

Who actually benefits from this ego thinking? That large house with all those bathrooms will cost you an extra $5,000 a year in taxes when compared to that two-bedroom house. Over the life of a thirty-year mortgage, you will pay an extra $150,000 in real-estate taxes. All your utility bills will triple, and all the money you could have saved for vacations or retirement goes in someone else's pocket.

The bankers love this ego message. They know the average person can't do math. For instance, just a modest $1,000 a month payment you make on a $100,000 mortgage will mean you give the bank $360,000 for that $100,000 loan. (1,000 × 12 months × 30 years). Every dollar in down payment will save you three dollars over the life of the loan, and a twenty-year mortgage will save you thousands more over the life of the loan. When you put no money down and take a thirty-year mortgage, the bank ends up with all the money you could have saved; the banker really appreciates your generosity.

And that bigger house is going to cost you much more than you think. When you reach retirement and that big house requires an extra $5,000 a year in taxes and double utility bills, how is your social security check going to cover those expenses?

Another math problem your banker hopes you'll never notice is the 12 to 18 percent interest you pay on your credit cards every month. Credit cards can become an addiction similar to that uncontrollable compulsion to do drugs. Those thousands in interest you pay the banker are helping him put his kid through Harvard; what is your kid getting out of it?

There is an easy way to tell if you are following a good choice or a bad choice; just run the movie all the way to the end and see if the outcome seems to be in your own best interest.

There are many ways we can downsize and minimize, but we can't do any of them if the ego is in charge of our thinking. If I believe I need to do things to impress others, then that belief means others are telling me who I am and how I should live. Then I become their slave.

The 1% are never going to pay attention until they feel the results of the message that the rest of us can send by refusing to allow them to manipulate us out of our hard-earned money. If the 99% change, the 1% has to change whether they like it or not.

The things described in chapter 12 can be done by anyone who sees the wisdom in not being a victim. I can make these changes without anyone noticing that I have taken charge of my own self-care.

"A crust of bread eaten in peace is better than a banquet served in adversity." (OT Proverb)

Socrates Said, "You are taught that money and extravagance are the means for happiness. Yet the gods need nothing. Therefore I choose to live closer to the gods."

In our next chapter, we are going to become a little more active in our belief in the Gandhi Principle. The use of noncooperation and nonviolence does not mean we give up our right to employ active self-expression.

AN EFFECTIVE WORLD COURT

Governments controlled by the 1% cannot build their ego-inspired empires without the use of military intimidation. The same intimidation that has destabilized the entire world for the last ten thousand years and made the lives of the 99% unpredictable and subject to the manipulations of the ego.

If the 99% refuse illegal military service, the 1% can no longer intimidate anyone. We need to use the Gandhi Principle in order to reform the ego behavior of the 1%. Instead of the tail wagging the dog, the dog returns to wagging its tail as nature intended.

The ego has been running the show for eons, but things are changing. This is the age of communication; it's no longer easy for the 1% to remain in the shadows and plot their mischief.

Changing the status quo will have to be done in steps. The refusal of military service will be the first signal to current governments that the 99% are no longer going to be victims of the ego. The ego will react to this threat, but in a later chapter, we will be specific as to how to defend your constitutional right to refuse illegal military service. (The life you save may be you own, and your neighbor's.)

This boycott of military service will stay in place until an effective world court is organized and proven to be effectively operating. (The current World Court is a good start, but it needs the ability to enforce the rules including the ability to nullify diplomatic immunity in cases of indictment for criminal behavior.)

This effectiveness is not difficult to accomplish when a sane majority no longer chooses to live in the lawlessness of the Wild West dominated by a minority of insane egos.

The establishment of an effective court needs to begin with the realization that there will be governments that refuse to participate. (Similar to when the Wild West gunslingers were asked to check their guns at the sheriff's office before entering town.) This is an easy problem to solve because sane people outnumber the insane people.

A world court that only requires a vote of 75 percent of the participating countries to indict someone for "crimes against humanity" " can easily overcome the objections of any rogue gunslinger. The necessity for this 75 percent provision is realized when we see the ineffectiveness of the current U.N. to prosecute war criminals. This ineffectiveness is the result of the U.N. requirement to obtain 100 percent approval of all the members of the Security Counsel before they can take action. This provision requiring 100 percent agreement translates into allowing the 1% to control the 99%. This is how the 1% has been able to effectively neuter the U.N. and continue to use war as a means to make money and control empires.

The ego disguises this UN design flaw by delegating the major function of the UN to humanitarian assistance. The ego knows that if its true nature were exposed to the light of day, no one would tolerate it. So it uses humanitarian aid as a cover story. This is a true catch-22. The ego creates the wars that cause the crisis and then provides the humanitarian aid to clean up the very mess it created.

This is why the only effective way to stop this insanity is for the 99% to refuse military service until an effective world court is in operation.

The Wild West will continue to be wild until the gunslingers can be brought to justice in a court of law.

Historians claim that the UN could not have evolved without the 100 percent agreement of all its members. The obvious explanation for the inclusion of this crippling rule originates with the motivation of those who wrote the provision; all of them were not willing to subject themselves to a truly effective process because they were controlled by the 1%. This is also why the 99% have to boycott military service until the rules are improved. It's the Gandhi Principle.

It is not necessary, or even possible, to have every government on the planet agree to an effective court. All that is necessary is for a majority of sane governments to agree. These governments are going to be encouraged by the 99% who do a sit-down strike against war. Someday the 1% will start a war, and the 99% won't show up.

As a practical example, let's say the court indicts a head of government or corporation and subpoenas him or her to appear for trial, but he or she refuses to comply. The court responds by issuing a warrant for his or her arrest, and if the offenders are caught outside their borders, they are taken into custody and tried. In other words, the offenders are no longer free to travel outside their home country. It's similar to house arrest.

In addition, anyone involved in helping these individuals avoid extradition is subject to arrest for obstructing justice. This is why the word "effective" is necessary when describing a world court.

This process of extradition is limited to crimes against humanity and unrelated to any particular country's internal laws for other infractions. These infractions already have an internal process for litigation and do not need duplicate or an overlapping process of prosecution. This provision removes a nation's ability to abuse or complicate the system.

A) Whose National Sovereignty

For decades the ego-controlled governments objected to submitting themselves to a truly effective worldwide legal system because they claimed it interfered with their national sovereignty.

The dictionary tells us that the word sovereign is related to the concepts associated with royalty. It appears that the belief in the divine right of kings is still with us; the ego depends on it. And until the 99% refuse to submit to the king's abuse, royalty will rule while the subjects suffer.

The ego is confident that the peasants are incapable of challenging its control; this is the illusion that exposes the ego's insanity and its disconnect from reality. In chapter 12, we described how the effectiveness of the Gandhi Principle overcame the ego illusion of British imperialism. This refusal to cooperate with tyrants has been proven to be an effective means for making them disappear, but it will only work if the 99% are willing to work it.

The belief in the Divine Right of Kings has faded into history and attempts to replace it with the concept of national sovereignty are scheduled to experience the same fate. It took centuries to dethrone the king, and it may take a similar interval of time to dethrone the ego, but time is no match for eternity. The ego's days are numbered.

B) Have You Heard the Joke about Gun Control?

How can gun control advocates be taken seriously when we never hear them say one word about controlling the international arms business—a secret enterprise that kills millions of innocent men, women, and children?

Politicians who talk about controlling the guns owned by Joe the plumber or Mack the mechanic know that it's safe to target the little people, but exposing the illegal business of international arms dealers is off limits. There is big money connected to this business, and politicians are afraid of anything associated with big money.

Have you ever heard the name of an international arms dealer broadcast on the eleven o'clock news? You are never going to hear that information, because major network news is owned by corporations—the same corporations that are involved in the international arms trade.

I recall watching an amateur, iPhone video of a column of modern tanks being driven down the street by an army of terrorists—terrorists who were using those made-in-America tanks to kill American soldiers. This is how the term "Military-Industrial Complex" takes on a whole new meaning when the country you are sworn to protect is also supplying the equipment that is going to kill you.

Those American tanks being driven by terrorists are not going to appear on the eleven o'clock news; instead, an altered version of a few rebels riding in a pickup truck and shooting AK-47s in the air is chosen for broadcast. This corporate-controlled news employs the mushroom method of "keep 'em in the dark and feed 'em manure." This kind of edited news is all you will ever see on your TV because it's controlled news, or sometimes, deliberately misleading news.

Do you know what the abbreviations API and UPI stand for at the end of those stories you read in your evening newspaper? They represent the Associated Press International and the United Press International. These organizations collect the stories submitted by reporters all over the world and then someone sitting in an office decides which stories will go out on the wire to appear on the evening news or in the newspapers. Have you ever noticed how the daily news sounds the same no matter which TV or radio broadcast you listen to? It's because the wire service decides what is available for broadcast. This kind of edited news is quite similar to being censored news.

Knowing how this edited news system works also has a positive implication; it illustrates how iPhones and the Internet are going to put an end to decades of mind control. The days of the ego are numbered. But don't think the ego is going to give up without a fight. The ego has been addicted to money and power for hundreds of years and will get desperate when its drugs of choice dry up.

This is the very reason that the Gandhi Principle is the most effective way for starving the Bad Wolf; don't cooperate with the Bad Wolf, and he will get weak and fade.

It is also a mistake to believe that physically attacking the Bad Wolf will accomplish long-term change. History is littered with physical revolutions, but the ego eventually reappears. This is why the establishment of an effective world court is necessary; it's the first step toward a permanent solution for taming the Wild West; no more gunfights in the street will be tolerated.

The new court will enforce new laws regulating the international arms business. Only manufacturers who have court-approved licenses can participate. All armaments will have identification numbers traceable to the manufacturer. Any unauthorized use of these armaments will result in sentences of life in prison for the user and the manufacturer. This is an incentive for the manufacturers to keep accurate, traceable records of all legal business transactions and also to report the theft or misappropriation of their equipment. Any unlicensed manufacturing or use of unlicensed armaments is also subject to life imprisonment for the user and the manufacturer.

It is naïve to believe that guns are going to disappear, but it is not naïve to believe they can be more effectively regulated.

The ego will not be concerned with the threat of these new regulations. It has been running a secret, and often illegal, arms business for decades. But denial is blocking the ego's ability to see a major flaw in its belief that it can continue with business as usual. All addicts deny there are eventual consequences for continuing their addiction. That's the function of denial—the disconnect from reality.

When the 99% refuse military service, there will be no more soldiers to operate the equipment and consequently no market for the equipment. The final curtain will begin to descend on those who fail to comprehend the ending of the old Wild West and the beginning of the new age of reason.

C) Natural Selection

As the ego-controlled people who are currently in power read this book, they smile with confidence that they will always maintain control. This ego perception is an illusion because they are looking through mouse eyes. They believe that because they have controlled their kingdoms for an entire lifetime, this achievement is evidence that their beliefs are correct. This mouse-eye view is their undoing.

In contrast, Eagle Eyes look ahead with confidence and know that the ego will disappear because Eagle Eyes see time and natural selection through Spirit-guided perception.

Spirit-guided people see the wisdom of the Gandhi Principle and therefore refuse to participate in the military insanity of mass murder. In contrast, the ego-guided people will volunteer to be cannon fodder for the ego-directed Military-Industrial Complex. This is because ego-guided people have an affinity for one another, they all see through mouse eyes. This ego-directed decision by these volunteers results in death, and their DNA is removed from the gene pool.

This process of one group following Spirit perception while the other group chooses to follow the ego is an easy lesson in natural selection; the DNA of the ego-directed people will eventually disappear from the gene pool as the DNA of the Spirit-directed people becomes the new species. Through this process of natural selection, the ego follows the dinosaurs into extinction.

D) Insanity Costs Money

The Military-Industrial Complex and the church of the ego continue to increase the national debt by their constant use of lies to justify our military and religious intrusions into other people's lives. It is interesting how last decade's Godless communism has been switched to this decade's attack on "Moslem terrorists." The religious tone of these descriptions betrays the presence of the church of the ego. But it has become necessary to omit the label "Godless" because the Moslems worship God, but the church of the ego claims that it is not the correct God. This delusion is just another example of the ego's reliance on denial; Moslems, Jews, and Christians are all people of the same book. They all claim a common ancestor, Abraham. Consequently, they are all cousins of the same great-great-grandfather, but the ego hates to acknowledge this oneness through its use of denial.

The same ego denial is revealed in the misuse of the word anti-Semitic. Conventional use of this word suggests it means anti-Jewish, but the dictionary tells us that both Jews and Arabs are Semitic people. This is logical because Arabs and Jews both have the same great-great-grandfather. This semantic error is another example of how the ego promotes separation while the Spirit teaches unity.

Separation leads to attack, and unity leads to peace; this is an observable fact.

In our next chapter, we will examine specific ways for implementing the Gandhi Principle and why it's becoming the most important necessity of the twenty-first century.

THE CONSTITUTION

Very few people are aware of the detailed history of what indigenous people call the trail of tears. It began with the decision to roundup all the Indians living in the Eastern United States in order to remove them to the Indian Territory west of the Mississippi River. If only one of your parents were native, you were included in the deportation. Many of these Indians had farms and businesses, but everything they owned was confiscated. Many died on this long walk.

The major portion of this injustice occurred between 1830 and 1845. But the point of mentioning this particular stain on American history concerns the attitude displayed by President Jackson.

Attorneys for the Natives won an injunction in the Supreme Court to halt this unconstitutional action by the federal government. When Jackson was informed of the court's decision, he ignored it by saying, "That may be their opinion, let me see them enforce it."

This habit of ignoring the Constitution has been an ongoing problem ever since its inception in 1789. For an additional example, people who had an economic interest in continuing the practice of slavery refused to accept the constitutional principle of equality for all. Unlike Jackson, President Lincoln had the willingness and the power to defend the Constitution, and he did.

In 1920 women had to actively protest for their legal right to vote. It became necessary to add an amendment to the Constitution in order to clarify the fact that women were real human beings and should have been included in the original concept of equality.

This process of insisting that the provisions of the Constitution be honored and protected is an ongoing struggle.

The details described in article 1, section 8, of the US Constitution concerning the organization of national defense have been ignored and violated for decades. These violations are protected by political and economic interests that benefit from ignoring the Constitution. The future of democracy depends on correcting these violations. And, similar to the slavery question, these violations are motivated by economic and political gain without concern for protecting the Constitution.

This is why it is necessary for the 99% to invoke the Gandhi Principle until this error is corrected because the lords controlling the US government will never willingly give up their access to this illegal wealth and power.

Failure to protect the Constitution will ultimately lead to the bankruptcy of the nation and the disappearance of democracy. Then the 99% will be reduced to serfdom, and the lords will maintain complete control.

A) Nothing New under the Sun

The habit of subverting or ignoring the law is a favorite method employed by the ego to maintain power and wealth.

In chapter 7 of this book, we described how the Spirit told Moses that if the nation made the mistake of asking for a king, then the king would be required to abide by certain rules. He was not to acquire excessive wealth and was not to be exalted above other members of the community. This same chapter describes how Samuel was disturbed when the people eventually asked to have a king, and the Spirit gave Samuel a warning to deliver to the people concerning the abusive things the king would inflict on the community.

The people ignored the warning and history records the consequences that the Spirit correctly predicted.

It's informative to examine the Jewish community's motivation for ignoring this Spirit warning.

In the beginning of the Exodus from Egypt under the inspired leadership of Moses, every able-bodied man was required to defend the community against assault. There wasn't a select group of individuals composing a separate army; the whole community was involved.

This provision requiring everyone to participate provided an incentive to avoid conflict; no one intentionally chose to start an unnecessary war because they would all have to be involved.

This rule of having everyone involved in community defense is the opposite of what the Israelites observed in the pagan nations. These nations had kings, and these kings had specific armies that went out to battle while the rest of the community sat safely at home out of harm's way. On the surface this arrangement of letting someone else do the fighting had a certain appeal even if it ignored the Spirit's warning.

The logic of the Spirit is revealed when we understand the wisdom of this law. When every member of the community is exposed to the potential hazards of war, it provides an incentive to use diplomacy rather than bloodshed in order to settle disputes.

The opposite effect takes place when the king has sole power to use his private army for acquiring personal wealth by stealing it from the neighbors.

These two opposing conditions illustrate the difference between Spirit-directed wisdom in contrast to ego-directed chaos.

The Spirit knows there are no true winners in attack and mutual murder. The ego believes the opposite; it thrives on attack as the primary means of satisfying its addiction to power and wealth.

A careful reading of article 1, section 8, of the US Constitution reveals how the composers of this document understood the wisdom of requiring every member of the community to be involved in the common defense. They also set limits on the duration of raising a Federal Army. This limit is necessary in order to protect the Treasury from bankruptcy.

I believe it is informative to understand the requirements of article 1, section 8, in order to have legal reasons to refuse military service as long as the Constitution is being violated. If someone is arrested for refusing military service for these reasons, it will present an opportunity to litigate this issue all the way to the Supreme Court and thereby put an end to ignoring the Constitution.

There are three provisions described in article 1 for protecting the nation against foreign invasion.

One: section 8, paragraph 13, says, "Congress is to provide and maintain a Navy." This navy is the only permanent and continuous provision for the federal government's involvement in direct military defense.

The composers of the Constitution understood that a foreign invader could not complete the invasion and occupation of the United States without employing the naval transport of troops and equipment. This is why there is a provision for maintaining a permanent navy.

Modern technology has added an additional deterrent to foreign invasion with the deployment of nuclear-armed submarines. These naval submarines are capable of delivering nuclear retaliation for any offshore assault on our nation.

Two: section 8, paragraph 15, says, "Congress is to provide for calling forth the Militia to execute the laws of the Union, suppress insurrection, and repel invasion."

The terms "militia" and "army" are not interchangeable. Careful reading of the provisions for these Militias reveals how each State in the Union is to have a well- regulated Militia as an internal defense against invasion. If the adult population of all the combined state militias provided ten million troops for national defense, it would be military suicide for any foreign force to attempt to set foot on American soil. (See Switzerland's version of the effectiveness of this militia concept described in Gwynne Dyer's book *War*.)

This concept takes us back to the Spirit requirement of having all citizens responsible for the community's defense. This provides an incentive for avoiding unprovoked military intrusions across international borders—intrusions that are the imperialistic adventures of the ego and have nothing to do with national defense.

The concept of "repelling invasion" in paragraph 15 is in no way related to our police actions of the 1950s and 1960s in Korea or Vietnam.

Politicians claim we had treaty obligations and were obligated to defend them. This excuse of treaty obligations is a thin disguise for attempts to install military bases on the border of China. This selective use of the treaty excuse is exposed by the US government's failure to explain why we don't have treaties to protect democracies in South America. We are in fact guilty of subverting legally elected democracies in South America.

Rhetoric is an interesting means for manipulating words, but when the rhetoric is illogical, the words become meaningless. The ego is cleaver, but it is never truly logical. If this comment of rhetoric seems confusing, it may be helpful to ask Native Americans how they perceive the validity of the word treaty.

Three: section 8, paragraph 12, says, "Congress can raise and support armies, but no appropriation of money to that use shall be for a longer term than TWO YEARS." This limit of two years indicates that the Constitution prohibits the long-term development of a Federal Army. National defense is delegated to the well- regulated militias of the various states.

Provisions throughout article 1 describe how the federal government is to partner with the states in order to ensure that the organization of national defense is uniform with a consistent and organized plan for maintaining an orderly chain of command.

Limiting the long-term use of Federal Armies is intended to prevent a permanent drain on the US Treasury. This is why President Eisenhower warned the nation of the danger of allowing the continuous development of the Military-Industrial Complex.

In chapter 3, the reader was asked to use the Internet to review the military budgets of all the major nations on the planet. These bar graphs give stark evidence as to how the structure of the Federal Military is bankrupting the country. The annual expenditures for the Pentagon average between one-half and three-quarters of a trillion dollars. Since 2002 the illegal wars in Iraq and Afghanistan have cost the American taxpayers over $8 trillion (that is an eight followed by twelve zeros).

The politicians who benefit from supporting the Military-Industrial Complex are constantly saying we need to increase defense spending and cut social services. Does that $8 trillion figure suggest we need an additional increase in military spending?

Comparisons of the bar graphs of the United States, China, Russia, England, Germany, France, and so on reveal how the US military budget dwarfs all the rest of the countries in the world.

Politicians have been known to add provisions to the military budget that the military generals say they don't need or want. This waste and extravagance illustrates how politicians are controlled by the corporations who profit from these unnecessary expenditures. It is all about money and has nothing to do with true national defense.

B) Eggs in One Basket

The attempt to use fear in order to keep public attention focused on national defense is a slight-of-hand ego trick to divert attention away from better and less expensive solutions. The development of an effective world court would require considerably less money when compared to the costs associated with war and the preparations for war. This is why the first order of business for effecting true change requires the 99% to invoke the Gandhi Principle, and not to participate in military service until an effective world court is in place to prosecute war criminals. Then and only then, will the organization of national defense, as defined by the Constitution, be implemented. To reverse this order of priorities will do nothing to correct the overall problem of making war a profitable business for the 1% at the expense of the 99%.

Unless the 1% who promote conflicts are put in jail or removed from the illegal arms business, the addiction of the ego to money and power will continue to expose the 99% to the chaos of the divine right of kings.

The ego is insane, and if it is allowed to continue its reckless and illegal behavior, the 99% will continue to be its victims. The only true solution to this problem is to refuse to participate. The Gandhi Principle has proven that it is effective for defeating tyrants, but it won't work unless the 99% are willing to work it.

C) The Beginning

Chapter 10 of this book describes the illusory experience of the multiplex theater. It also describes how the Spirit inserts pieces of truth into the movie scripts in order to lead the mind out of the illusion and into the light of reality. This book is merely a piece of that process. All over the planet, there are people waking up to the Voice of the Spirit. It is a soft voice and therefore does not attract attention. But there is no need for It to attract attention because It has all the time in the world to complete Its assignment. God is love and has arranged for everyone to win.

Doak—sha.

SUGGESTED GOOD BOOKS

The Disappearance of the Universe, by Gary Renard, 2002.
This book offers detailed information concerning everything you need to know in order to graduate from the Earth School. The second most important book you will ever read. Gary describes the most important book.

Journey of Souls, by Dr. Michael Newton, PhD, 1994.
This book explains everything you need to know about how the Earth School really works.

The Last Hours of Ancient Sunlight, by Thom Hartman, 1998.
A brilliant analyses explaining why renewables are the only long-term solution for maintaining modern society.

Healing Words, by Dr. Larry Dossey, MD, 1993.
This book is a collection of research examples of the mind's function in the healing processes.

The Conscious Universe, by Dr. Dean Radin, PhD, 1997.
This book contains the meta-analysis of experiments that demonstrate how humans have mind abilities that are not being used.

War, by Dr. Gwynne Dyer, PhD, 1985.
> This book describes the history of war. The evolution and motivation for war hasn't changed. Only technology makes it appear different.

Future Shock, by Alvin Toffler, 1970.
> The predictions in this book have arrived; unfortunately, few people paid attention.

The majority of these books were published decades ago. They help illustrate how true wisdom and insight never go out of style.

July 2017.